KT-520-941

POTATO RECIPES

PRICE
3D

For Me it's—
UP·IN·THE
MORNING
AND·FIT
ALL·DAY!

That's the feeling that makes life worth living. You just enjoy everything because you feel healthy and fit. That is the natural condition.

If you feel shaky, nervous or depressed; if you can't sleep or enjoy your meals; if your will for work is weak — your system is disordered. You need Dr. Cassell's Tablets. They will put new life into you, tone up overtaxed nerves, and give you increased strength and vigour.

Take

Dr. Cassell's Tablets

The great tonic and energiser,
And always be fit.

1/3 and 3/- per box. Of all chemists and stores.

MAKE A
JELLY "LILY POND"
as a surprise dish for Sunday

Very easily prepared
with

CHIVERS JELLIES

Here's the very latest Chivers recipe, "Jelly Lily Pond" —what a wonderful surprise for everybody at your table if you serve it this week-end. You could scarcely imagine a more attractive dish and yet just notice how easy and inexpensive it is to prepare. Why not cut out the recipe now, you'll want to use it for Sunday. But Chivers Jellies are too good to be kept for special recipes only—serve them often in everyday meals. You see Chivers Jellies contain real fruit juice — that's why they are so good for everybody, especially at this time of the year. Order a few packets from your grocer NOW.

Chivers Jellies for cool, sparkling sweets

CHIVERS & SONS LTD. THE ORCHARD FACTORY HISTON CAMBRIDGE & MONTROSE SCOTLAND

HOW TO MAKE
Jelly "Lily Pond"

1 pkt. Chivers Jelly (lemon or greengage)
2 or 3 oranges, 1 banana
A few cocktail sticks, Angelica
Cocoa powder (or chocolate)

Make jelly in usual way and set in shallow glass bowl, reserving ¼ pint. Cut oranges in halves and scoop out pulp—cut cleaned skins to resemble water lily (see illustration). When cool whisk ¼ pint jelly to stiff froth, fold in orange pulp and fill into orange skins. Place these on the jelly in bowl. Cut from banana a few small pieces, roll in cocoa powder, pierce with cocktail sticks, and arrange with angelica at the side of bowl to appear as bulrushes.

CHIVERS JELLIES

No. 5
MACDUFF'S
SCOTTISH FOODS OF QUALITY

METHOD: Sufficient suet should be put into deep frying pan to cover well the food to be fried. The temperature should then be raised until a piece of white bread dropped in turns golden-brown in half a minute. Tis temperature is reached without the appearance of any unpleasant fumes usually associated with frying.
Coat the fish with egg and seasoned bread crumbs, or dip into a frying batter. Fry the fillets in deep suet. Drain the fish well, put on a hot dish, garnish with parsley and slices of lemon: serve very hot.

Fillets of Fish

...made Sweets
Treacle Toffee

THIS is the old-fashioned treacle toffee which most people have forgotten how to make. The necessary ingredients are: 1lb. treacle, 1lb. white sugar, 1lb. margarine, 2 tablespoonfuls water, 1 tablespoonful vinegar. Boil all these together for 25-30 minutes until a few drops, when dropped into cold water, become crisp. Stir frequently when boiling. Pour into a buttered dish.

J. M.

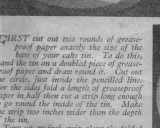

Goodfellow & Steven

BROUGHTY CASTLE

SCOTCH SHORTBREAD

PRODUCT OF SCOTLAN[D]

A CAKE TIN

You Will Need Grease-proof Paper, A Pencil, A Ruler And A Pair Of Scissors.

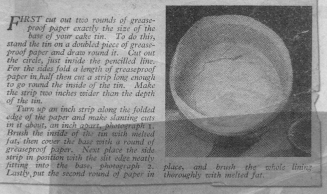

FIRST cut out two rounds of grease-proof paper exactly the size of the base of your cake tin. To do this, stand the tin on a doubled piece of grease-proof paper and draw round it. Cut out the circle, just inside the pencilled line. For the sides fold a length of grease-proof paper in half then cut a strip long enough to go round the inside of the tin. Make the strip two inches wider than the depth of the tin.

Turn up an inch strip along the folded edge of the paper and make slanting cuts in it about an inch apart, photograph 1. Brush the inside of the tin with melted fat, then cover the base with a round of greaseproof paper. Next place the side strip in position with the slit edge neatly fitting into the base, photograph 2. Lastly, put the second round of paper in place, and brush the whole lining thoroughly with melted fat.

OMELET MAKING.

Use a small pan for an omelet of 2 or 3 eggs, or the correct thickness cannot be obtained.

. . . . .

Use a steel, aluminium or tin pan, but never an enamelled pan, or the omelet will stick. It is best to keep a special pan for the purpose. See that it is absolutely clean and free from any burn.

. . . . .

A pliable cook's knife is required to fold the omelet.

. . . . .

Have everything prepared before mixing: an omelet is not improved if it is kept in the pan while the dish is heated or the garnishing prepared.

. . . . .

Do not beat the eggs very much. Do not allow them to stand or they will become thin.

. . . . .

Use fresh butter for omelets. Salt butter will make them stick.

. . . . .

The butter should be hot, but neither smoking nor burning, when the eggs are added.

Maw Broon's

Cookbook

A Gift to My Dear
Daughter-in-law, Maggie, on
her Wedding Day

Jeannie Broon

P.S. Enjoy yer big day,
lassie!

Published 2007 by Waverley Books, an imprint of Geddes & Grosset,
David Dale House, New Lanark, Scotland ML11 9DJ

Text copyright © 2007 Waverley Books and DC Thomson & Co Ltd.
Maw Broon, The Broons logo and supporting characters appear courtesy of, and are copyright © 2007 DC Thomson & Co Ltd. Selected newspaper and magazine clippings are from the Sunday Post archive and are courtesy of DC Thomson & Co Ltd.
Design, setting, and editing by Waverley Books and Gran'maw Broon.

All rights reserved. No part of this publication may be reproduced, stored in a retrieval system or transmitted in any form or by any means, electronic, mechanical, photocopying, recording or otherwise, without the permission of the copyright holders.

The rights of Gran'maw Broon and Maw Broon tae be identified as authors of this work hae been asserted in accordance with sections 77 and 78 of the Copyright, Designs and Patents Act 1988.

Conditions of Sale
This book is sold with the condition that it will no', by way of trade or otherwise, be re-sold, hired oot, lent, or otherwise distributed or circulated in any form or style o' binding or cover other than that in which it is published and without the same condition being imposed on the subsequent purchaser eh? An' if it is taken oot o' Maw's scullery drawer it is to be put back efterwards or ye'll get a thump on the lug.

A' the recipes in this book were supplied and tried by Maw Broon, Gran'maw Broon, and freens and neebours, but Maw and the publisher cannot be held responsible for any that go wrang or if ye dinna follow the instructions right or dinna pay attention to modern food hygiene rules.

ISBN 13 : 978-1-902407-45-6   Printed and Bound in the EU

Acknowledgements
For permission to use their trademarks, thanks to: Tunnocks; Goodfellow & Steven; Unilever (Bovril); Heinz (HP Sauce); Wilson's of Kendall (Duncan's Hazelnut); G R Wright (Imperial Plain Flour); and Chivers.
  The trademarks Bird's Custard, Atora, Bisto and Oxo are used by permission of Premier Ambient Products (UK) Limited. Van Houten and Van Houten's Cocoa are registered trademarks of the Barry Callebaut group and are used with permission.
  Every effort has been made to contact the copyright holders of material reproduced in this book. However, if you believe your copyright has been infringed we would like to hear from you at: Waverley Books, David Dale House, New Lanark, ML11 9DJ.

Dear Maggie,

Welcome tae the family. This book is a collection o' recipes that my ain mither passed tae me, an' there's bits an' pieces that have come my way from freens and neebours ower the years. It's food fur week days, high days an' holidays. Ye'll find a' the recipes that your man is familiar wi' in here.

I've ca'd it 'Maw Broon's Cookbook'. That's me ye know — but ane day that'll be you! There'll be a family, Maggie, I'm sure — ane or twa bairnies tae keep ye busy. Ye'll hae yer hands full if my ain life has been onything tae go by!

An' ye'll hae your ain favourite recipes an' a' — frae your ain mither mair than likely — but you are a Broon noo, an' you'll no' go far wrang wi' the recipes in this book.

Paw, bless him, has looked oot a few bits an' bobs frae oor kitchen drawer that might come in handy. Ye can pick them up when you come roond tae visit. Just a few pots an' pans an' the like.

Well, I'll leave you tae it !

With much love,

Jeannie × × ×

3

Oven temperatures

Granmaw's old recipes don't give specific oven temperatures. The range never had temperature settings. This is roughly what is meant by 'quick' and 'hot' and 'moderate' etc. Hope I got the gas marks right.

Very Slow	= 225–275°F	110–140°C	gas mark ½ – 1
Slow	= 300°F	150°C	gas mark 2
Slow Moderate	= 325°F	160°C	gas mark 3
Moderate	= 350°F	180°C	gas mark 4
Quick Moderate	= 375°F	190°C	gas mark 5
Moderately Hot	= 400°F	200°C	gas mark 6
Hot	= 425–450°F	220–230°C	gas mark 7–8
Very Hot	= 480–500°F	240–260°C	gas mark 9

GARDINER'S Herbs

Cicely, Sweet
Myrrhis odorata.

COMMON NAME: smooth cicely, British myrrh, anise, great sweet chervil, smelt chervil, sweet brack, sweet-fern, sweet humlock, sweets, the Roman plant, shepherd's needle, cow chervil.

OCCURRENCE: native to Great Britain and also found in mountain pastures across Europe.

PARTS USED: the root and herb.

MEDICINAL USES: aromatic, carminative, stomachic, expectorant. The fresh root may be eaten or used as a tonic in brandy. It eases coughs, flatulence, indigestion and stomach upsets. The herb, as an infusion, is good for anaemia and a tonic for young girls. The antiseptic roots have been used for snake or dog bites while the distilled water is diuretic and effective in treating pleurisy. Sweet cicely essence is said to have aphrodisiac properties.

ADMINISTERED AS: a root infusion, herb infusion, decoction, essence and distilled water.

GARDINER'S Herbs

Sunflower
Helicanthus annuus

COMMON NAME: helianthus, marigold of Peru, Sola indianus, Chrysanthemum peruvianum, Corona solis.

OCCURRENCE: native to Peru and Mexico and was introduced into America, Europe and Great Britain as a garden plant.

PARTS USED: the seeds. These contain a vegetable oil, carbonate of potash, tannin and vitamins B1, B3 and B6. The oil is expressed from the crushed seeds and, according to the range of temperature to which the seeds are heated, several grades of oil are obtained.

MEDICINAL USES: diuretic, expectorant. It has been used successfully in treating pulmonary, bronchial and laryngeal afflictions as well as whooping cough, colds and coughs. The leaves are used, in some parts of the world, to treat malaria and the tincture may replace quinine in easing intermittent fevers and the ague. Sunflowers produce the seed cake which is used as cattle food; the fresh leaves are given to poultry; the plants can be used as a vegetable; the stems are used as bedding for ducks; the plant used for silage, fuel, manure, textiles and as a soil improver.

ADMINISTERED AS: sunflower oil, tincture, decoction, poultice.

GARDINER'S Herbs

...ops
...us lupulus

...tive in ...from ...t is ...species ...nd in ...orthern

...the ...n volatile ...n-ciples- ...inic acid-

...ES:
...diuretic,

The volatile ...soporific effects while the bitter principles are ... Hops are used to promote the appetite and ... infusion is very effective in heart disease, fits, ...on, jaundice, nervous disorders and stomach or ...op juice is a blood cleanser and is very effective ...ulus problems. As an external application, hops ...CHAMOMILE heads as an infusion to reduce ... or in-flammation and bruises. This combination ...d as a poul-tice.

...ERED AS: an infusion, tincture, poultice, ...ture or tea.

Contents

Daphne ate all The pies

Temperatures

Gas Mark	°F	°C
	32	0
	50	10
	100	40
	122	50
	212	100
1	275	140
2	300	150
3	325	160
4	350	180
5	375	190
6	400	200
7	425	220
8	450	230
9	475	250

Liquid Measures

Unit		fl oz	ml
teaspoon	1/3 tbsp.	1/6 fl oz	5 ml
tablespoon	3 tsps.	1/2 fl oz	15 ml
cup	1/2 pt.	8 fl oz	240 ml
fluid ounce	1/16 pint.	1 fl oz	30 ml
1 pint	32 tbsps	16 fl oz	480 ml
gill	1/4 pint	4 fl oz	120 ml
quart	2 pints	32 fl oz	960 ml
1/2 pint	16 tbsps	8 fl oz	240 ml
1/4 pint	8 tbsps	4 fl oz	120 ml
1 1/4 pint	5 gills	20 fl oz	600 ml
1 3/4 pint	7 gills	28 fl oz	840 ml
2 pints	1 quart	32 fl oz	960 ml
1 litre	4 1/2 cups	2 pt 1 fl oz	1000 ml
gallon	4 quarts	8 pt	3840 ml

Dry Weights

Imperial	Metric (exact)	Metric (based on 1oz=25g)
1/8 oz	3.5 g	3 g
1/4 oz	7 g	6.25 g
1/2 oz	14 g	12.5 g
1 oz	28 g	25 g
2 oz	57 g	50 g
3 oz	85 g	75 g
4 oz	113 g	100 g
5 oz	141 g	125 g
6 oz	170 g	150 g
7 oz	198 g	175 g
8 oz	226 g	200 g
9 oz	255 g	225 g
10 oz	283 g	250 g
11 oz	312 g	275 g
12 oz	340 g	300 g
13 oz	368 g	325 g
14 oz	396 g	350 g
15 oz	425 g	375 g
1 lb	453 g	400 g
1 1/2 lb	680 g	600 g
2 lbs	900 g	800 g
2 1/2 lb	1134 g	1 kg
2.3 lb	1 kg	—

Handy Measures

1 rounded tablespoonful flour or other powder	1 oz.	25g
1 level teacupful flour or other powder	4 oz.	100g
1 rounded dessertspoonful "	1/2 oz.	12g
1 rounded teaspoonful "	1/4 oz.	6g
1 teacupful sugar, rice, etc.	6 oz.	150g
1 level tablespoonful sugar, etc.	1 oz.	25g
1 level dessertspoonful sugar, etc.	1/2 oz.	12g
1 level teaspoonful sugar, etc.	1/4 oz.	6g
1 teacupful grated cheese	3 oz.	75g
1 teacupful bread crumbs	2 oz.	50g
1 tablespoonful treacle, syrup, or jam	2 oz.	50g
1 piece of fat the size of a small egg	1 oz.	25g
1 piece of fat the size of a walnut	1/2 oz.	12g
Therefore, a wee dod o' butter is …	1/2 oz	12g
1 piece of fat the size of a hazelnut	1/4 oz.	6g
Therefore, an awfy wee dod o' butter is …	1/4 oz.	6g
1 breakfastcupful liquid	1/2 pt.	240ml
1 small teacupful liquid	1/4 pt.	120ml

Maw, I have rounded these up and
down to make it easy. If you don't mix
metric and imperial measures in the same
recipe it will be fine,

Horace

7

Quantities of Food Per Person

Soup	1/2 pt. and 1/2 pt. over.	1/2 pint is 240ml
Fish	4-6 oz.	100-150g
Meat	3 oz.	75g
Vegetables	2-4 oz.	50-100g
Potatoes	2 20 FOR Daphne Maw, tell them!	
Milk Puddings	1 gill	A gill = 1/4 pint = 120ml
Steamed Puddings	2 oz.	50g
Scones and Buns	2 oz.	50g
Cakes	1 1/2 oz.	37g
Tea	1 teasp. and 1 over (up tae 4 persons).	

Measurements	
Inches	Centimetres/Millimetres
1/8	3 mm
1/4	6 mm
2/5 (0.39)	1 cm
1/2	1.3 cm
3/4	1.9 cm
1	2.54 cm
2	5 cm
3	7.6 cm
4	10 cm
5	12.7 cm
6	15.2 cm
7	17.8 cm
8	20.3 cm
9	22.8 cm
10	25.4 cm
11	28 cm
12	30.5 cm

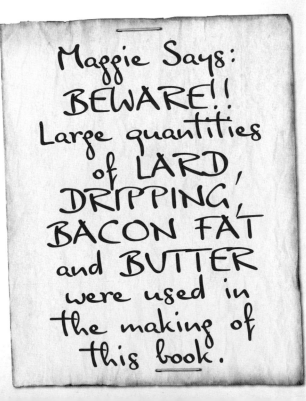

Maggie Says: BEWARE!! Large quantities of LARD, DRIPPING, BACON FAT and BUTTER were used in the making of this book.

Basic Cooking

Tae start ye aff, I've written oot a' the
recipes I think a new Broon should ken,
an' these will serve ye weel when
ye hae yer ain family.

Types of Cooking

Boiling

General Rules:

Fresh meat—Put into boiling water, boil 5 minutes, then simmer.

Salt meat and fish—Put into cold water. Bring to boil. Pour off water. Cover with boiling water, then simmer.

Fresh fish—Put into boiling water. Cook just under boiling point.

Vegetables—Put into boiling water (exception, old Potatoes). Boil quickly.

Steaming

Rules:

1. Make all preparations, and choose a pan with a tight-fitting lid.
2. Have sufficient boiling water to come half-way up bowl containing food.
3. Bowl should only be two-thirds full.
4. Water must be kept boiling (except for very light mixtures such as custards).
5. If necessary add more boiling water.

Stewing

Rules:

1. Choose a pan or jar with a well-fitting lid.
2. Have sufficient liquid to come half-way up food.
3. Boil for 5 minutes then simmer gently.

Frying

There are two methods:—

1. Shallow Frying.—Use sufficient fat to come half-way up the food.
2. Deep Frying.—Use sufficient fat to cover the food entirely. This method is suitable for small cuts of tender meat, fish, vegetables, fruit, reheated dishes, etc.

Rules for frying:

1. Make all preparations.
2. All articles to be fried must be thoroughly dry, and should be coated if necessary.
3. Have fat smoking hot and have sufficient for the purpose.
4. Do not put too many articles in the pan at once.
5. Reheat fat between each batch.
6. Drain thoroughly and serve at once.

cut here ✂

Porridge

A warming and sustaining morning meal

1.2 litres/ 2 pints water
50g / 2 oz medium oatmeal
50g / 2 oz coarse oatmeal
full fat milk or cream
salt

Bring the water to the boil and sprinkle in all the oatmeal, stirring continuously. Lower the heat and **simmer** for about 20–30 minutes, depending on how thick you want the mixture to be. Season with a large pinch of salt and serve with milk or cream. Although salt is best to bring out the flavour of the oats, honey, syrup and molasses are also perfectly acceptable and traditional additions to porridge.

Serves four

Housewife Weekly
"cut out and keep"
Scottish Recipes No. 17

To keep food hot
Instead of putting food into the oven to keep it hot for late-comers, try covering it closely with a tin or plate, and setting it over a saucepan of hot water. This plan will keep the food hot, and at the same time prevent it from drying.

To keep a larder sweet
Place a pan of charcoal in it, for it helps greatly to keep everything sweet and wholesome.

Porridge

Maggie, my laddie needs a guid breakfast every day or he gets awfy crabbit. He'll be wantin' sassidges every day if he can get awa' with it. But he'll appreciate the sassidges mair when he gets them if you mak' him porridge mair regularly. When your family comes along, oats will go further than butcher meat and they're filling. This recipe is enough for twa folk.

1 cup of pinhead oatmeal (or course rolled oats)

3 cups of cold water

Salt

Milk

Soak the oatmeal overnight in water (if yer using rolled oats then there is nae need tae dae this). The following day, add a guid pinch of salt and bring the oatmeal slowly tae the boil. Stir continuously with a spirtle and serve when thick and creamy. Serve with full-cream milk and a further sprinkling of salt. Yer man likes jam on his, the wee sowel!

Bread Sauce

2 ozs. breadcrumbs,
1/2 pint milk
8 peppercorns, crushed
Blade mace

1 onion
1/2 oz. butter
Seasoning

Simmer the onion, peppercorns and mace in the milk. Strain and stir in the breadcrumbs and butter. Add seasoning, and simmer for about five minutes, till the crumbs have soaked up the milk.

Housewife Weekly "cut out and keep" Scottish Recipes

cut here ✂

No.21

Oatcakes - Perfect with cheese, butter, honey or jam

100 g/4 oz coarse oatmeal
100 g/4 oz medium oatmeal
100 g/4 oz fine oatmeal or barley meal
1/4 teaspoon baking powder
1/2 teaspoon salt
25 g/1 oz butter or dripping, melted
4 to 7 teaspoons boiling water

Preheat the oven to Mark 4/ 300°F/150°C. Mix the oatmeal. Put 250 g/9 oz of the oatmeal, the baking powder and salt into a bowl and stir in the melted butter. Slowly add the hot water to make a smooth, firm paste.
Form into a ball and roll the mixture on a table sprinkled with 25 g/1 oz of the remaining oatmeal. Ensure the mixture is completely covered with oats and roll out into a circle about 1/2 cm (1/8 inch) thick. Cut into 8 wedges. Using a fish slice, transfer the wedges on to a baking sheet covered in the remaining oatmeal.
Bake in the centre of the oven for about 30 minutes withoutallowing to brown.

Makes eight oatcakes

White, or Foundation, Sauce

A white sauce can be turned intae a' manner o' things and it's jist braw wi' biled vegetables or on champit tatties. If ye can mak' a guid white sauce it will serve ye weel.

1 oz. butter

1 oz. flour

1/2 pint liquid (milk, water, or fish or meat stock)

Melt the butter in a saucepan. Add the flour, mix thoroughly and cook for a few minutes. Add liquid gradually, beating well, add seasoning; stir till boiling point, cook five minutes, or until the flour is a' cooked out.

Sauces ye can mak' fae foundation sauce:

Melted butter sauce — add 1 extra oz. butter

Onion sauce — add 2 large onions (chopped, sweated)

Mustard sauce — add 1 teaspoon mustard (made)

Parsley sauce — add 1 tablespoon chopped parsley

Sweet Sauce — add (tae an a'-milk sauce) 2 teaspoons sugar, a wee drap flavouring.

13

Betty's Ovenless Bread

This was awfy useful when my oven broke, much love, Auntie Betty x x x

8 oz. flour
4 level tsps baking powder
Pinch of salt
2 oz. butter
1 1/2 gills milk or milk and water

Sieve the flour, baking powder and salt. Rub in the butter. Stir in the milk. Roll on a floured board to 1/4 in. thick and make into a round. Place on a greased, hot girdle and bake on top of the stove until well browned and puffed up. Turn. Serve hot, spread with butter.

14

Yeast

Tests for freshness:
1. Compressed yeast should be pale fawn in colour.
2. It should have a fresh smell.
3. It should be firm but crumble easily.
4. It should become liquid when creamed with a little sugar.
5. If there are dark spots, it means that some of the yeast has died and the dough will not rise.
6. Small quantities of yeast will keep fresh for several days if pressed into a jar and covered with a cloth wrung out of cold water. Leave the jar in a cool place.

Points to note when using Yeast:
1. Yeast should be fresh.
2. Keep everything warm. Yeast needs warmth so that fermentation can take place. Excessive heat kills yeast growth. Cold retards it.
3. Small quantities of dough require more yeast than large quantities.
4. To raise and bake a dough quickly, more yeast is required than if a longer time is allowed for rising.
5. More yeast is required to raise rich doughs containing fat and eggs.
6. Too much sugar will prevent the yeast from growing properly.
7. Too much salt will prevent the yeast from acting quickly.
8. Fat slows up the action of yeast.
9. Less liquid is required if eggs and fat are used.
10. Water should be boiled and milk scalded before use to destroy any germs. They should then be cooled until lukewarm before using.
11. Self-raising flour should not be used.
12. Proportions vary with the recipe and method of mixing. Follow the recipe carefully.

Breid

White Breid	Broon Breid
3 1/2 lbs. flour	3 lbs. wheaten, 1/2 lb. white flour
3 teaspoons salt	3 teaspoons salt
1 1/2 pts. tepid water	2 oz. lard
1 teaspoon sugar	1 oz. yeast
1 oz. yeast	1 teaspoon sugar

Mix the flour and salt. Add sugar tae the yeast, mix until creamy and then add warm water. Mix with the flour and knead till ye hae a smooth elastic dough. Cut across surface of dough in 4. Cover bowl with towel and set aside in a warm place until the dough is double its original size (1 1/2-2 hours). Knock it back — knead thoroughly tae distribute gas. Shape into loaves, place in warmed tins, cover and let it rise again (15 minutes). Bake in a hot oven 5 minutes, then reduce heat and bake 1/2—1 hour, according tae size of loaf.

Mrs Gow's Mince Collops

1 lb. minced lean steak
1 oz. butter
1 onion, chopped
1 teacup of strong beef stock
Salt and pepper
Sippets of toast
4 poached eggs

Trust her to try to be fancy with mince

Melt butter in a saucepan and saute onion till soft. Add mince and stir with fork till browned. Add stock and simmer for one hour. Add salt and pepper and taste before dishing. Pour onto a hot dish. Then make 4 poached eggs. Place on the mince and garnish with sippets of buttered toast. Serves two.

To Make Mince Spin Out

1 lb. mince
1/2 lb. pinhead oatmeal
2 big onions (or 3 medium)
3 carrots, diced
2 ladles of beef stock or gravy
2 big handfuls fresh green peas
Plenty of seasoning, sage, pepper and salt or mixed herbs

Brown the onions and the mince. Add the carrots and stock and oats. Cook 1 hour. Add peas and seasoning, and serve once peas cooked.

16

WHIT'S A COLLOP? IS IT LIKE A DOLLOP?

Maggie's Mince with Mushrooms

1 lb. steak mince
1/4 pint stock
A small onion, chopped
2 oz. butter
1/2 oz. flour
12 mushrooms
Pepper and salt
6 or 8 triangles of toast

Fry the onion in 1 oz. butter. To this add flour and stock, the steak mince, four of the mushrooms minced, and seasoning. Simmer for 3/4 hour. Fry the remainder of the mushrooms whole in the rest of the butter. Make the toast. Place a mushroom on each piece of toast. Place these all round an ashet and pour the mince in the centre. Voila!

Trust HER to try to be fancy wi mince an a'!

Mince and Tatties

Mince and tatties are a Broons staple. I hae a special mince pot that I will pass on tae ye when I am gone (no fur a while yit!).

1lb mince

2 onions chopped

A dod of butter (1 oz)

2 carrots chopped

1oz plain flour

Beef stock or gravy   thank goodness for gravy powder

Cook the onions in butter in the pot till soft. Add the mince, mash it tae separate the pieces and then brown it. Chop the carrots into circles — they taste best this way — and add tae the mince. Add the flour and mix thoroughly. If ye hae beef stock or gravy add enough tae cover the mince. If not, ye can add water but mind to season well as it will no' be sae tasty. Cook till mince is tender and carrots are soft and the gravy is nice and thick — about an hour. Add a wee bitty water if it is too thick. Serve with mashed tatties and butter.

17

BREAKFAST RECIPE
by Hen Broon

Ingredients: Fried tattie scone, fried soda scone, fried tatties, fried bacon, twa fried eggs – sunny side up, scrambled eggs, sausages, Lorne sausage, black pudding, mealie pudding, fruit pudding, an' BROON sauce.

Method: Cook and eat.

Serve with: Toast an' butter an' jam an' strong tea wi' three sugars – or a can of Irn Bru – or lager!

BRAW!

BREAKFAST BAPS

These baps, or morning rolls, are the perfect accompaniment to a hearty breakfast.

450 g/1 lb strong plain white flour
2 level tsps salt
50 g/ 2 oz vegetable fat or butter
15 g/ 1/2 oz dried yeast
1 tsp caster sugar
125 ml/1/4 pint milk
125 ml/1/4 pint tepid water

Sieve the flour and salt, and rub in the fat. Mix together the yeast, caster sugar and water. Heat the milk until it is lukewarm and then add it to the yeast mixture. Gradually add the liquid to the flour and knead to a soft dough for about ten minutes, or until you feel the dough becoming elastic. Place in an oiled bowl and cover with cling film. Leave the bowl in a warm place for an hour, or in a cool place overnight.

Turn the dough out of the bowl, knead it lightly and divide into around seven ovals. Place them on a greased baking tray, cover and leave to prove in a warm place for a further 30 minutes.

BRUSH WITH MILK AND DUST WITH FLOUR AND PLACE IN THE OVEN AT 220°C/425°F/GAS MARK 7, FOR 15 TO 20 MINUTES

✂ cut here

Housewife Weekly
"cut out and keep" Scottish Recipes

50 g/2 oz fat, dripping or butter
3 onions, chopped
1 kg/2 lb floury potatoes (such as Maris Piper), peeled and sliced
250 g/1/2 lb cooked lamb or mutton, with gravy or stock reserved
1/2 small turnip, diced (optional)
3 medium carrots, sliced (optional)
salt, black pepper, ground nutmeg

Stovies - Some variations include the addition of beef, lamb or fish – but all include the potatoes being cooked slowly on the stove

No.11

Melt the fat and cook the onions. Lower the heat and slice the potatoes in varying sizes. Add the potatoes and cook for 10 minutes on a low heat, stirring occasionally. Add a little stock, gravy or water and then the carrots and turnip. Cook until the potatoes are soft. Add the strands of cooked lamb and heat through. Taste and add seasoning.
Serves approx. three to four

Stovies

Mutton is the Broons' favourite for including in stovies, but it could be made with any meat. Ye'll find different versions of stovies in different books and fae different folk — nobody cooks it quite the same way. That Mrs Gow puts sausages in hers but I dinna like that.

2 tablespoons dripping

1 1/2 lb tatties, sliced

1 onion, chopped

2 carrots, sliced

half a small neep

2 tablespoons stock or meat jelly

4 oz lamb, cooked

Salt and pepper

Lamb stock

Melt the dripping in a large pan and cook the chopped onion in it until softened and almost brown. Add the chopped tatties and mix thoroughly with the onions and dripping. Add the chopped carrots and neep and mix through. Heat the stock or meat jelly and pour over the vegetables. Add the chopped, cooked lamb and mix with the vegetables. Season with salt and pepper. Cover the pot and cook over a low heat for around 30 minutes or until the tatties are soft and floury.

Scrambled Eggs

I know ye'll know how tae mak' this, Maggie, but I thought I'd mention my laddie's fussy ways. He hates scrambled egg that has been overcooked and has separated — the toast gets wet! If he moans tae me aboot it I jist say, "Mak it yersel'!" I suggest you dae the same!

4 eggs mixed with 4 tablespoons milk
1 oz. butter

Mix the eggs and milk, and season with salt and pepper. Melt the butter in a saucepan and pour in the egg mixture. Stir ower gentle heat till the mixture thickens. Remove frae the heat immediately once thickened or the mixture will separate. If ye're feeling flush, miss oot the milk and use extra butter instead — then ye dinna hae tae worry about the liquid separating.

Egg Cookery

Boiled eggs — Add to boiling water, simmer 3-4 minutes.

Hard-boiled eggs — Boil for around 10 to 15 minutes. Leave in cold water to avoid discolouring.

Coddled egg — Good for invalids — Pour boiling water over a fresh egg and leave at side of stove for 6 minutes.

Poached egg — Break egg into cup, and slip gently into boiling salted water. Simmer until set, remove from pan, drain.

Scrambled egg – Mix 4 eggs well with milk. Cook gently in butter in a saucepan till thick. Overcooking will cause the eggs and liquid to separate.

Housewife Weekly
"cut out and keep"
Scottish Recipes

No.28

Potato Scones
Tasty savoury scones –
ideal served hot for breakfast

Mash potatoes until smooth and add a generous pinch of salt and the butter. Mix in the flour, kneading with the hands if necessary, but do not let the mixture become too dry. Roll out thinly and cut into triangles. Brown on both sides on a griddle or frying pan. Serve hot, spread with butter.

500 g/1 lb floury potatoes,
     mashed
salt
100 g/4 oz plain flour
50 g/2 oz butter

WHITE BANNOCKS
OR SODA SCONES

1 lb. Flour
3/4 teaspoonful Bicarbonate of Soda
1/2 teaspoonful Salt
3/4 teaspoonful Cream of Tartar
1/2 pint Buttermilk

Sift all the dry ingredients together into a baking bowl, holding the sieve up high to get as much air into the mixture as possible. Mix to a soft dough with the milk. Roll out on to a floured board and divide into four rounds each about half an inch thick. Cook on a hot girdle for five minutes and turn over. Lower the heat and finish cooking them for a further five minutes.

Emdring
        Quaker Oat Biscuits
4 oz butter.
2½ tablespoons golden syrup
2 oz. sugar.
½ lb rolled oats (Quick Quaker)

Cream butter & sugar, melt
syrup in pan, add to butter & sugar
Put in oats last & mix well.
Quick oven for about 5-10 mins
            until brown.

22

Potted Hough

My man and your man baith love potted hough. I love it tae.
Ask the butcher for the shin of beef.

1-lb hough of beef (shin)	1/2 mace blade
2-lb beef shin bone or	1/2 teaspoon peppercorns
knuckle of veal	1 bay leaf
1 teaspoon salt	Salt
1/2 teaspoon allspice berries	Pepper

Place the meat in a large, thick-bottomed pan and pour in
enough cauld water tae just cover it. Tie the bay leaf and spices
in a piece of muslin and add this tae the pan. Bring tae
the boil and then reduce the heat and simmer for three tae
four hours. The meat should be awfy tender by now. Drain the
stock fae the pan but dinna throw it awa'. Flake the meat
fae the bone and shred or chop it finely. Place the stock and
meat back in the pan and taste tae see if ye need tae add
additional salt and pepper. Boil again for anither 10 minutes
or so tae mak' sure there is no' ower much liquid. Pour the
mixture into wee moulds or bowls and leave tae cool completely.
Chill. Serve wi' breid or oatcakes.

Cullen Skink

A delicious fish soup

1 onion, sliced or chopped
3 or 4 crushed peppercorns
butter
water
1 medium Finnan haddie
(salted smoked haddock)
500 g/1 lb (approx.) potatoes
600 ml/1 pint milk
salt and pepper

Fry the onions with some butter and the crushed peppercorns. Add the fish, cover with water and cook until the skin becomes loose enough to remove. Remove the skin and break the fish into flakes, removing the fish bones as you do this. Put the haddock aside and return the skin and bones to the pan and simmer for about an hour to make a stock.

Boil and mash the potatoes. Strain the fish stock, add to a large pan and simmer with the milk. Add as much potato as you like, depending on whether you prefer thick or thin soup. Add the flaked haddock. Season with salt and pepper and perhaps some butter.

Serves approx. three to four

Housewife Weekly
"cut out and keep"
Scottish Recipes

No.27

Handwritten notes:

SKink? ThaT'S jUST daf T

Cullen is small fishing village on the shores of the Moray Firth and skink means soup or stew.

OoooOooooh!!!

---

1 kg/2 lb mutton
(flank or shoulder)
1.8 litres/3 pints cold water
50 g/2 oz barley, washed
25 g/1 oz dried peas
salt, black pepper
75 g/3 oz carrots, chopped
75 g/3 oz turnips, chopped
50 g/2 oz onions, chopped
75 g/3 oz leeks, chopped
50 g/2 oz kail, chopped
11/2 tablespoons parsley, chopped

Mash potatoes until smooth and add a generous pinch of salt and the butter. Mix in the flour, kneading with the hands

Housewife Weekly
"cut out and keep"
Scottish Recipes

Scotch Broth
A traditional, filling broth

No.41

if necessary, but do not let the mixture become too dry. Roll out thinly and cut into triangles. Brown on both sides on a griddle or frying pan. Serve hot, spread with butter.

Soup

As well as the recipes before, the best thing ye can learn how tae mak' well is soup. I don't trust a woman who cannae mak' soup, Maggie. I'm sure your mother has taught ye weel though. It's the simplest thing, and if money is tight it is a Godsend for feeding your family.

Your man likes a guid Scotch Broth best.

I

Stockless Soup

This is much nicer than it sounds!

2 big onions, chopped finely
2 oz butter
2 pints of the salted liquor in
which vegetables have been boiled
2 or 3 slices of stale bread
Handful bacon rinds
Plenty of pepper

Fry the onions in the butter. Add
the vegetable water. Add the bread
and bacon. Simmer for an hour.
Pass through a fine sieve. Reduce
and add milk. Season and serve.

Blellgh! —>

WHEN MAKING SOUP —

When making soup choose a strong deep pan with
a tight-fitting lid.

Chop your vegetables finely and sauté them in a
little butter first.

Use cold water to draw out the full goodness.

Cook the soup slowly and simmer — do not boil.

You can make soup out of any vegetable if you
follow these rules.

Vegetable stock always tastes best if you include
celery.

Bone Stock

Raw or cooked bones

4 pints cold water

Salt

2 carrots, chopped

1 wee turnip, chopped

Onion, chopped

2 sticks of celery, chopped

Wash the bones and cover wi' cauld water. Add 1 teaspoon salt tae each two pints of water. Bring slowly tae boil, and spoon aff scum. Add the chopped vegetables when stock is half cooked. Bone stock should boil steadily for 5 hours. Strain and use. Some say that the bones could be used again for a second stock but I find that the flavour is mostly lost. (Gie them to yer neighbour's dug!)

Daphne's Tomato Soup

1 lb. tomatoes (fresh) sliced
1 1/2 pints chicken or vegetable stock
Salt and pepper
1 oz. butter
1 onion
Half a cup of milk or cream

Very slimming! If you miss oot the cream ... and the butter ... and the chicken stock.

Put tomatoes in pan with the onion, seasoning, and butter, and sweat them for 20 minutes; add stock, and simmer till tender. Sieve. Add half a teacupful of hot milk or cream.

Slimming-class times:

Monday 8pm – too late
Wednesday 8:55am – too early
Thursday 6pm – cookery class clashes
Saturday 9am – er ...

daphne

Eggs

Icing Sugar
T. Puree
C. Flour

Tattie Soup

This is ane o' my favourites. Very economical, and delicious.

8-10 tatties

1-2 onions

2 carrots, grated

A mutton bone

4 pints water

Salt and pepper

1 tablespoon chopped parsley

Early in the day, wash the mutton bone and put it into a pot with cold water and salt. Follow the recipe on the previous page for bone stock. Bone stock needs to cook for 5 hours, mind. Wash, peel, and slice the tatties. Wash, scrape, and grate the carrot. Peel and cut up the onion. Remove the bone and strain the bone stock. Add the vegetables to this stock in the pot, and simmer for 1 1/2 tae 2 hours. Wash and chop the parsley, and add tae the soup richt at the end. Season, and serve.

ITALIAN SOUP

1/2 lb. Turnips
1/2 lb. Carrots
1/2 lb. Onions
1/4 lb. Macaroni
1 small Beetroot
1 oz. Parsley
2 oz. Butter
2 quarts Water
1 pint Milk

Slice vegetables (except the beetroot), and boil them in water; break the macaroni small and boil it in the milk. When the vegetables and macaroni are cooked, mix them, add parsley and beetroot previously boiled and cut small, butter and seasoning. Heat thoroughly and serve.

KIDNEY SOUP

1 Ox Kidney
1 tablespoonful Beef Extract
2 Carrots
2 Spanish Onions
Pepper and Salt
1 oz. Roast Dripping,
3 quarts boiling Water

Remove all fat from kidney, cut in slices, and flour it well. Put it into a pot with the dripping, stirring till well browned. Then add the boiling water and onions, cut in quarters, and pepper and salt. Let all simmer for 3 or 4 hours. Skim off the fat, add the carrots, grated and the beef extract, and serve hot.

OXTAIL SOUP

An Ox Tail
2 oz. Dripping
2 oz. Flour
3 Onions
1 Carrot
1 Turnip
tops of stalk of Celery
a little Thyme (either dried or fresh)
Pepper and Salt
3 quarts Water.

Cut tail in pieces. Slice onions, and cut carrot and turnip into dice. Put dripping in frying-pan, and stir in flour as dripping melts. Then put in vegetables and stir for 5 minutes. Add meat, and fry for 10 minutes, stirring occasionally. Turn all into pot and simmer 3 hours, skimming well. About an hour before serving put in shreds of celery, thyme, peppers and salt. May be strained and thickened with 1 tablespoonful flour. Serve small pieces of tail in the soup.

OYSTER SOUP
(Made from a stock of Cod's Heads)

For 1 pint of white stock:
2 Cod's Heads
1 teaspoon Salt
A small piece Carrot
A small Turnip
1 onion
Parsley
12 peppercorns
1 blade mace
2 cloves
12 Oysters
1 gill Oyster liquor
A little Salt
1 tablespoonful Corn-flour
1 gill Milk
1 pinch Pepper (cayenne)
1 squeeze Lemon Juice

Put 2 cod's heads into a pan with enough cold water to cover them, add the seasoning and vegetables. Boil for 2 hours; strain stock; let it stand for 2 hours. Remove all fat.

Add the oyster liquor to the white stock and heat. Mix pepper and milk, and stir till it boils. Take off heat. Simmer gently. Add lemon and oysters. Do not let soup boil after oysters are added. Serve with diced fried bread.

Hough Soup

2 lb. Hough (Shin of Beef),
4 pints Water,
2 Onions,
Salt and Pepper.

Take marrow from bone and place in pot. When hot, put in meat cut small, and simmer 5 minutes, stirring occasionally. Add water and onions cut small, and boil 3 hours. (This same recipe without the onions and a knap-bone added makes good potted meat.)

maw,
Horace says he loves cod's heads and could he have them for a special Tea just for him

Celery Soup

Margaret Purdie gave me this ane. When Mrs Gow comes tae visit I cook this. She thinks it's something richt fancy, but I never let on that it isn't really, because it tastes lovely. This is simple, but rubbing it through the sieve is hard work. Get yer man tae dae this — it is his faither's job in oor hoose.

2 heads celery

1 oz. butter

4 pints chicken stock

1 potato, grated

1/4 pint cream

Salt and white pepper

Wash and cut up the celery, and sweat (or 'sauté' if ye are Mrs Gow) with the seasoning in butter for about 20 minutes. Add stock, grated tattie, and simmer till celery is tender. Rub through the sieve and return tae the pan. Taste, add seasoning and simmer. Just before serving, add some cream. Serve wi' diced toasted breid ('croûtons' if it's for Mrs Gow).

31

Hotch Potch

This is a grand recipe, Maggie. I think it is even better than Scotch Broth.

Love, Auntie Betty

2-3 lbs. neck of lamb on the bone
1 1/2 pints fresh green peas
1/2 pint broad beans
1 cauliflower, in sprigs
6 small turnips, diced
6 carrots, diced
6 small onions, chopped
6 sprigs parsley, chopped
5 pints water

Put the neck of lamb into a pot with the cold water and a little salt and draw it through the boil. Skim off any scum. Keep half a pint of peas, and put the rest of the vegetables into the boiling liquid. Draw to the side and simmer for three or four hours. Half an hour before serving, add the cauliflower to the broth with the remainder of the peas. Just before serving add the parsley.

Beef Tea

This is guid for giving to your weans or auld folk if they are feeling poorly — it's full of goodness. Beef tea shouldna be boiled, just gently simmered.

1 lb. very fresh lean beef
1 pint cold water
Pinch of salt

Wash the meat and dry it. Slice the beef as finely as possible with a sharp knife, taking oot ony gristle. Lay it tae soak in a pint o' cauld water wi' a guid pinch of salt for twa hours, then turn into an earthenware jar, cover with a plate, and place in a saucepan of boiling water, where it should simmer gently for 3 tae 4 hours. Mind and stir it now and then. Strain and add a wee drappie salt and pepper.

Anither method is tae pit the jar in a slow oven instead o' the saucepan o' boiling water.

TREACHEROUS DAYS
Don't take cold — take BOVRIL

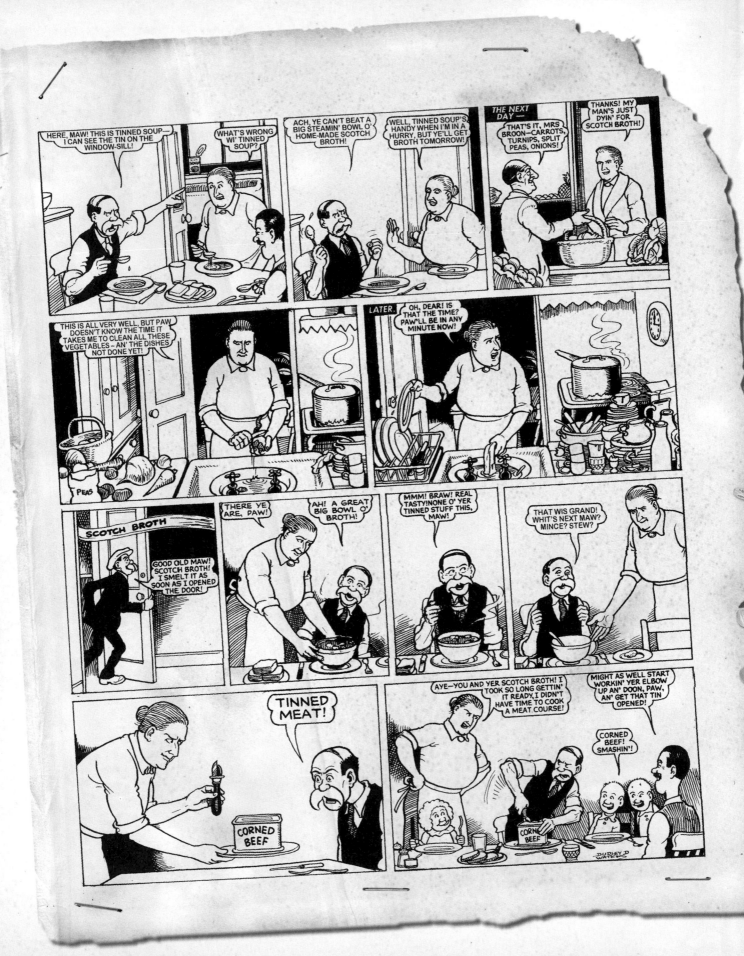

Scotch Broth

This is my laddie's favourite. The broth can be made wi' beef instead o' mutton. Wi' beef, the vegetables should be: kail instead o' white cabbage, twa sticks o' celery instead o' the parsley, and a bit mair leek. The meat should be removed when ready, and returned tae the pot later tae heat through.

1 1/2 lb. neck of mutton	1/2 heart of cabbage
2 oz. barley	1 cup diced neep
2 oz. dried peas	2 medium carrots, diced
1 oz lentils	1 carrot, grated
1 onion, chopped	Salt and pepper
1 leek, sliced	4 pints water

Wash the peas and lentils and soak overnight. Sauté the onion in some butter. Wash and trim the meat, and place in a pot. Add water, peas, lentils, barley, and salt. Bring tae the boil and skim. Add the leek, neep and diced carrot. Simmer slowly for three tae fower hours. Add the cabbage, shredded, and grated carrot, and simmer another hour. Just afore serving, add some chopped parsley and pepper and salt if needed.

Feather Fowlie

1 chicken, jointed, soaked in salted water for half an hour
A slice of ham
A pot-posy (or 'bouquet garnis' if you're posh) containing: sprigs of parsley, thyme and a blade of mace
1 onion, chopped
1 stick of celery, chopped
1 tbsp parsley, chopped
Salt and pepper
2 pints water
1 cup chicken stock
1 tbsp cream

Put the chicken in a pot with the ham, celery, onion, herbs, and water. Cover, bring to the boil; then simmer for 1 1/2 hours. Strain, and remove the fat. Return the soup to a clean pan, and add the stock. Then add the parsley and some of the white meat of the chicken. Remove from the heat and stir in the warmed cream. Serve immediately

Lentil Soup

I prefer it made with a ham hough!!

1 lb. lentils
1 small turnip
1 onion, chopped
2 leeks, chopped
2 carrots, chopped
4 pints cold water
1 sprig parsley, chopped

Soak the lentils overnight. Next day, boil the water and add lentils and chopped vegetables. Boil for 2 hours. Sieve, and return liquid to pot. Add pepper, salt, chopped parsley just before serving. Serve with sippets of toast.

sippets — how genteel!

Cock-a-Leekie Soup

This can be made with an auld boiling fowl, and the flesh can be used in anither dish. Ye can miss oot the prunes but they're traditional. Me, I'm no fussy aboot having prunes in my soup!

3-lb chicken with giblets

1 bay leaf

1 lb leeks, chopped

4 pints water

1 oz rice

4 oz soaked prunes, sliced into strips

Salt and pepper

In a large pot, place the whole chicken, the giblets, water, bay leaf, green of the leeks and salt and pepper. Bring tae the boil and then simmer for 2 tae 3 hours. Pierce the flesh of the chicken tae mak' sure it's cooked. Tak oot the chicken, giblets and the bay leaf. Skim fat fae surface.

Add the rice, the white o' the leeks and the prunes and cook for 10 minutes. Remove some flesh frae the chicken, add tae the soup and cook for aboot 10 minutes mair.

ACCOMPANIMENTS TO FISH

Boiled fish — Lemon. White or egg sauce.

Fried fish — Lemon. White sauce.

Steamed fish — Lemon.

Salt fish — Egg Sauce.

Cod and hake — Hard - boiled egg, parsley or oyster sauce

Halibut, turbot and brill. — Lobster or shrimp sauce

Herrings — Mustard sauce

Soles — Melted butter or Dutch sauce

Whitebait and sprats — Cayenne pepper, pieces of cut lemon and thin slices brown bread and butter

Whiting and plaice — Melted butter and anchovy sauce

Boiled mackerel — When in season, gooseberry sauce, otherwise parsley sauce

Mullet — Oiled butter

Salmon — Green peas, cream sauce

Pittenweem fish man comes on Thursday, forenoon

Maggie loves his fresh mackerel and his freckles

Jealous, Daphne?

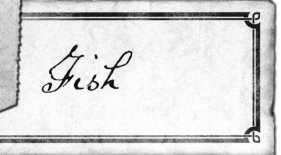

Fish

Your bairns will need tae eat up their fish to mak' them grow up clever. I don't know what happened to your man — I swear I made him eat up his herring religiously. My mother-in-law wasn't quite sae strict wi' her laddie.

THREE WAYS OF FRYING FISH

First Way — Fillet fish; wash and dry. Egg and bread-crumb.

Second Way — Dip first in milk, then in flour. Fat must be even hotter for this than when egged and bread-crumbed.

Third Way — Make a batter of flour, milk, a little salt, and tiny pinch of baking powder—about the consistency of thick cream. Dip the fillets in batter, and fry in a pan. Anything fried in boiling fat is puffed up and made very light by lifting it three or four times out of fat during the process. This lets in the air, and makes a great difference.

cut here

Housewife Weekly "cut out and keep" Scottish Recipes

No.14

A tasty shellfish soup-stew

3 dozen mussels in their shells, well scrubbed, beards removed
100 g/4 oz chopped leeks
50 g/2 oz chopped celery
50 g/2 oz chopped onions
600 ml/1 pint white wine or dry cider
300 ml/1/2 pint double cream
50 g/2 oz butter
chopped parsley
salt, pepper and nutmeg

Scrub the mussels thoroughly; discard any that are open. Bring the vegetables and wine or cider to the boil in a large pan and then drop in the mussels. Cook till they begin to open, then remove from the heat and cover for 10 minutes, shaking the pan occasionally until most have opened. Discard any that remain closed. Remove the mussels. Retain the stock, strain through a fine sieve and return it to the pan. Set the mussels aside. Taste the stock. Add the cream, butter, parsley and season with salt, pepper and nutmeg. Add the mussels in half-shells and heat them through.

Mussel Bree

Serves four to six

Grilled Scottish Salmon

A delicious, simple way to eat fresh Scottish salmon

No.33

wild Scottish salmon steak about 4 cm/11/2 inches thick
vegetable oil
25 g/1 oz butter, melted
chopped parsley
chopped dill
lemon juice

Dip the steak in melted butter or vegetable oil, sprinkle with salt and place under a hot grill until the flesh changes colour. Turn the steak and cook the other side. Serve with the central bone removed.

For a sauce, melt a little butter, add dill, parsley, a squeeze of lemon juice and pour around the steak. Serve with boiled potatoes and shelled or sugar-snap peas.

Serves one

Housewife Weekly "cut out and keep" Scottish Recipes

cut here

Frying fish

When frying, the temperature of the fat is important. Look for blue smoke before placing fish in the fat. When the temperature is right, a thin blue smoke will rise and the fat will become still.

****

Do not place damp fish in the fat. It will cause spluttering, and the fish will be sodden and unappetising. After washing, wrap it in a clean cloth, and if not using a batter or breadcrumb coating, dip it in flour before frying.

****

To make hard fat pure and free from sediment — after use, when cooled but still melted, clarify with boiling water. Pour over the fat and set aside for 24 hours. The sediment and bits of food will sink to the bottom, leaving the clean fat on top ready for the next frying.

40

Maggie, this is the way
my laddie likes it best —
but no' ower often mind,
or he'll put on the beef.

Fried Haddock

The batter recipe is Margaret Irvine's, who mak's the best fritters.

Four fillets of fresh haddock
A bowl of sifted flour with a pinch of bicarbonate of soda and
 a pinch of cream of tartar and a pinch of salt
Water (soda water if possible)
Malt vinegar
Enough dripping or hard fat tae fill a deep pan

Fry without a wire basket, because it will stick to it and lose the batter

Tae the flour, add the water gradually, whisking until the batter reaches a thick, bubbly creamy consistency. Add 2 tablespoons of malt vinegar (helps tae add tae the batter's crispiness).

Heat the fat in a deep frying pan. Dry the haddock fillets with a tea towel, then dip ane in the batter and coat it thoroughly. Immediately place it in the fryer. The fish will take between 5 and 10 minutes tae cook. Remove frae the fat, leave tae drain of fat in a basket, and keep warm in a hot oven. Dae the same with the rest of the haddock fillets.

41

How to prepare fish

Wash fish at the tap in running water.

Rub the black part of bone with salt, and scrape with knife

Remove the scales with the back of knife.

Wash in salt and water.

Skinning

Skin whitings and haddocks from head to tail.

Flat fish, except plaice, are skinned from tail to head.

In plaice the skin has to be peeled off with a knife.

Steaming and boiling fish

A spoonful of vinegar added to the water in which fish is boiling will make the fish firm and tender.

A pinch of bicarbonate of soda in the cooking water when boiling salmon makes the fish's flesh a lovely red colour.

Lemon juice is always an improvement to white fish.

Boiling is suitable for large uncut fish and for thick cutlets.

Steaming preserves the flavour of delicate fish.

Never skin a fish intended for boiling.

Generally speaking, fish should be cooked eight minutes to the pound and eight minutes over.

Cook gently.

Poached Finnan Haddies, from Mrs Gow

2 fillets of Finnan haddock

1/2 pint milk or enough to cover the fish in your pan

Freshly ground black pepper

1 oz butter

To a large frying pan add milk, ground pepper, a knob of butter and the haddies. Bring the ingredients slowly to the boil and cook until the flesh whitens and becomes tender.

Serve with some of the poached milk with brown bread and butter or floury potatoes

Nº 16

MACDUFF'S

SCOTTISH FOODS OF QUALITY

Ingredients: 1 haddock   Bread crumbs
Parsley   1 egg
Veal stuffing   1 oz. suet

METHOD: Thoroughly clean and dry the haddock, fill the inside with veal stuffing, sew it up and curl it round with the tail in the mouth. Put it in a well greased tin. Brush over with egg and strew bread crumbs over it. Put pieces of suet here and there over the top, and bake in a moderate oven for about ¾ hour. Baste often. Take out the string, and remove the fish to a hot dish with a fish slice. Serve with parsley sauce.

Stuffed Haddock

42

Arbroath Smokies

Smokies are haddocks, but unlike Finnan haddies they're smoked closed, tied in pairs by their tails. When I was a lassie and we visited my Auntie Nan in Auchmithie we aye brought smokies back wi' us. Auchmithie's first up the coast fae Arbroath — a richt bonnie wee place. Yer faither-in-law courted me there doon on the beach. He wiz aye jealous o' big Chic Gerrard the local fish lad!

1 pair of smokies
Butter

Preheat the oven tae medium-hot, or ye could use a medium-hot grill. Remove the backbone fae each fish by placing each on a flat surface, skin side down, and press along the length of the bone tae help loosen it fae the flesh. Ye can now remove the bone whole. Smear the smokies with butter and place on a tray in the oven or under the grill for aboot 15 tae 20 minutes. Serve with hot, buttered toast.

Betty's Fish Cakes

This micht be a way tae get thae fussy twins o' yours tae eat fish.

1/2 lb. cooked fish
4 ozs. tatties
2 ozs. butter, melted
2 eggs, beaten
Breadcrumbs
Dripping
Salt and pepper

Remove the skin and bones from the fish and flake it. Mix with tatties, butter, salt and pepper. Bind togeher with half the egg. Shape into round cakes. Brush the fish cakes over with remaining egg, toss in breadccrumbs. Heat the fat, very hot, in a frying pan. Fry the cakes to a golden brown. Serve immediately with green vegetables.

We like mince an' Tatties

Big Hoose Kedgeree

Ye ken that I like plain eating, I cannae be doing with you fancy spices. I can't see them catching on. But they made this up at the Big Hoose when I was in service and it was braw.

1/2 lb. cooked haddies or mackerel (flaked)
1/4 lb. boiled rice
2 oz. butter
Salt and pepper
1 tsp. curry powder
1 hard-boiled egg, chopped
Parsley

Melt the butter and add the seasoning and spices. Add the fish, rice and boiled egg. Garnish wi' parsley.

Fish Pie

Maggie, this fish pie can be made in advance — ye can hae yer man's tea ready an' keeping warm in the oven after his work and then you can go oot! He'll no' like that but he'll like the fish pie.

1/2 lb. cooked fish (flaked)
1 lb. mashed tatties
Salt and pepper
1/2 oz. butter
1/4 pint white sauce (see the recipe)
2 hard boiled eggs

Mak a white sauce, I've included a recipe at the front o' the book. Add fish and seasonings tae the white sauce. Chop the twa boiled eggs up fine and mix through. Pour the mixture into an ashet. Cover with smoothly mashed tatties and mark wi" a fork so that it browns more easily in the oven. Put a wee dod o' butter on top and bake in a moderate oven until browned (or Broon'd as we Broons say!).

Fried Herring

Yer man loves his fish and he loves tatties an' herring nearly as much as he loves a bit o' fried haddock. Fish is guid for the brain too — he needs it! We used tae hae fried herring a lot at Loch Fyne on oor holidays — lovely fresh fish.

Herring
Enough coarse oatmeal tae cover the fish
A pinch o' salt and pinch o' pepper per fish
Dripping, to fry with

Get the fishmonger tae gut the fish, remove the heads, fins and tails. Remove the scales, and wash. Dry thoroughly and score across on both sides. Then sprinkle wi' salt and pepper, and dip in coarse oatmeal.

Melt a wee bittie dripping in a frying-pan, and, when it is hot, fry the fish on baith sides, skin side first, until braw and broon (like me! I'm a Broon and I'm braw!). Serve hot with tatties and butter.

Stewed Pigeon

My faither kept doos when I was a lassie so I canny help feeling guilty when I make this.

2 pigeons
20 mushrooms
1/2 pint stock
1/4 lb. ham

Salt, pepper
1 oz. butter
1 tsp flour

Pluck and clean the pigeons. Slice and fry the mushrooms in a pan with butter. Add the pigeons and then the hot stock and seasoning to the pan. Add the chopped ham. Stew for 1–2 hours. Remove the pigeons, keep hot, strain and thicken the gravy with 1 tsp flour. Reduce, and strain over the meat.

Cooking Poultry

POULTRY and game may be preserved for a long time by tying a tight string round the neck to exclude the air and putting a piece of charcoal into the vent. A sprinkling of freshly ground coffee will keep game sweet for several days.

When stuffing a fowl which is to be roasted, insert the stuffing the night before and the flavouring will penetrate through the whole bird.

To clean a fowl, pick out all the pin feathers with the blade of a small knife, turn back the skin of the neck, loosening it with the finger and thumb, and draw out the windpipe and crop, which can be done without any cut.

Turn the fowl on its back and make a good, large cut just under the vent, and by working your fingers in slowly, keeping them close to the body, remove the whole of the bird's intestines in a mass, all the while being careful not to break the gall-bag, which is near the upper part of the breast-bone.

Wash the fowl thoroughly and dry it well with a clean tea towel. Put it in a deep roasting pan.

A very old fowl can be made as tender as a young chicken if cooked as follows:—Rub the fowl all over first with lemon juice, which whitens the flesh and improves the flavour. Then wrap in buttered paper and steam for 2 or 3 hours, according to size.

The flesh of an old fowl quite as delicious as that of a young one if cooked like this. The fowl may be roasted after being partially steamed.

Game and Poultry

Yer man and his faither will, noo and again, tak' tae 'hunting'. This generally means that they say they've shot some rabbits but they've really got them frae the butcher's.

I usually dinna let on that I know but try tae catch them oot later, it's mair fun.

From Mrs Gow: Gillies Venison Stew

Venison
Bacon fat or beef dripping
2 sticks of celery, chopped
1 onion chopped
Flour
Salt and pepper

Cut the meat into cubes and dip in seasoned flour. Melt plenty of dripping in a strong iron pot, put in the venison, and brown all over. Add the celery and onions. Season, cover closely, and cook gently for an hour or longer, until the meat is tender. Dish the meat, pour off the fat, and make gravy with some stock and the sediment in the pan, thickening it with flour. Serve with potatoes.

JUGGED HARE

1 hare, cut into egg-sized joints
3 oz butter
1 pint stock
1 wineglass port
2 finely chopped onions
1 stick celery
Juice of half a lemon
1-inch cinnamon stick, 4 cloves, 1 bay leaf, salt and pepper

Gravy:
The blood from the hare
2 level tsps arrowroot
Salt and pepper

Soak the pieces of hare in cold, salted water overnight. Drain and dry the pieces. Brown the joints evenly in a frying pan with butter. Pack them into the jug with the onions, celery, salt and pepper. Pour the stock and port over the meat, add the lemon juice, seasoning and cover the dish. Cook in a medium oven for two to three hours. Pour the gravy from the jug into a saucepan. Blend the arrowroot with water and then add to the blood. Simmer till thickened. Pour the gravy around the joints. Serve with forcemeat balls and red-currant jelly.

forcemeat balls, page 58

Roast Venison

It's no' often I get my hands on a nice bit o' venison, so when I dae, I want tae mak' sure it is cooked right. I dinna want tae add fancy flavours tae it — it's a strong flavour itsel'. It can be an awfy dry meat mind, so tak' care cooking it and gie it a langer time than mutton. Venison is awfy tasty browned and roasted in a pan ower the fire too — just cook slowly wi' a wee drappie stock or water. My mooth's waterin' just thinkin' aboot it, Maggie!

4 lb. venison

3 oz. dripping

1/2 pint milk or cream and 1/4 pint stock

Rub the meat a' ower wi' dripping. Roast in a covered dish in a hot oven. Baste the venison wi' milk or cream and when this is sooked up add the dripping and keep basting. When cooked, lift the venison tae a hot dish, pour awa' the fat, leaving the sediment in the pan. Add the stock, pepper and salt and a teaspoonful of red-currant jelly tae this. Stir it a' till it boils and strain over venison. Serve hot.

Stewed Rabbit

I remember greetin' cause my brither killed a rabbit and my mither made stew wi' it. Pair wee beastie! It tasted affy guid though, I soon got over it.

1 rabbit

2 ozs. butter

1 onion

Salt and pepper

3/4 pint stock

1 tablespoon flour

1/2 lb. fried bacon

Slice the onion and fry in 1 oz. butter in a thick-bottomed pan that has a good fitting lid. Clean and joint the rabbit (the butcher can do this). Wash and roll the flesh in seasoned flour. Fry in the ither ounce of butter amongst the onions. Add the hot stock, 1/4 lb bacon and simmer till tender. Remove joints, thicken the gravy. Strain gravy over the rabbit. Arrange wi' 1/4 lb bacon roon' the dish.

Rabbit Pie

Rabbit stew
1/4 lb. bacon, chopped
Rough puff pastry, see Granmaw's
    recipe

Put the rabbit stew frae the last page,
and the bacon, in a pie-dish. Cover with
a plate and place in a hot oven for about
half an hour to reheat. Remove the pie-
dish from the oven, allow it to cool,
then cover with the pastry. Bake for
another 1/2 hour.

STOVED GROUSE

A grouse, plucked and
    prepared
Sugar
Bacon fat

Melt a teaspoon of bacon fat in a frying-pan, and add a tablespoonful of sugar. Brown the grouse well in this mixture, turning it over often.

Then heat some bacon fat in a small stewing dish with a closely fitting lid. Put in the bird, cover, and cook on the top of the cooker for 1 1/2 hours, turning it over frequently.

Serve with roast root vegetables such as carrot and parsnip, game chips, skirlie and red-currant jelly.

The Scottish Grouse

Roast Grouse
(No jist for the toffs!)

Wi' ma man's hunting skills as they are, grouse has been a rare, rare treat in the Broon hoose. This is Mrs Gow's recipe, she says she eats it a' the time as her man is pally wi' a laird. Poaches it, mair like.

Grouse (a young bird)

Rashers of bacon

Butter, lemon juice, salt and pepper

Pluck carefully — grouse hae a delicate skin. Wipe inside and oot wi' a clean, damp cloth. Grouse is an awfy dry meat, so baste it with plenty o' butter that has lemon juice, pepper and salt worked into it. Put more of this inside the bird. Wrap the bird in rashers o' bacon and then in greaseproof paper. Place it, breast down, in a roasting-tin, and put it into a hot oven for 25 tae 35 minutes depending on the birdie's size. Ten minutes afore serving, remove the wrappings, flour the bird, and brown it. Serve with skirlie; chip potatoes, French beans, and clear gravy. Rowan jeely goes well wi' grouse.

Highland Hotpot

1 brace of grouse
1 rabbit
1/4 lb. streaky bacon
Head of celery, chopped
1/2 white cabbage, shredded
4 small onions, chopped
4 medium potatoes, sliced
Black pepper
Allspice
Salt
Stock

a brace of grouse is one male and one female bird

Prepare the grouse, and skin and gut the rabbit, and cut it into joints. Dip the joints in seasoned flour and brown in a frying pan. Slice the celery, onions and potatoes, and arrange with the grouse and rabbit in layers in a pot that can be used on the stove and also covered and moved into the oven. Fill about one-third full with stock. Bring to the boil, then add the cabbage and seasonings.

Cover the pot and transfer to a moderate oven and cook for two and a half hours.

Kingdom of Fife Pie

(Fowk in Fife are awfy proud o' 'Kingdom')

1 large rabbit or 2 small ones	Forcemeat:
1 lb. pickled pork	1 rabbit liver
Grated nutmeg	1 rasher fat bacon
Salt and pepper	4 oz. breid crumbs
1/4 pint stock	1 tablespoon parsley,
Forcemeat balls	1 tablespoon dried thyme, pinch
Rough puff pastry	grated nutmeg, salt and pepper
	Grated lemon rind
	1 egg

Skin and gut the rabbit, cut it into joints and wash them in cold water. Mak' a stock wi' the carcase and liver. Slice the pork. Mak' forcemeat balls from the rabbit's liver: chop liver and bacon, mix wi' the other ingredients, bind wi' egg, and make into balls. Season the rabbit, pork, and forcemeat with nutmeg, salt and pepper and place in an oven dish. Add the stock. Cover with rough puff pastry. Mak' a hole in the top. Put into a hot oven, but lower the heat to moderate and cook for 2 1/2 hours.

Forcemeat Balls

Forcemeat balls:
The liver from the animal

   4 oz streaky bacon

3 oz shredded suet

6 oz white breadcrumbs

1 tbsp chopped parsley

1 pinch dried thyme

1 pinch nutmeg

2 egg yolks

Make the forcemeat while your main meat is cooking. Mince the bacon with the liver and then mix this with breadcrumbs, herbs and spices. Bind this together with the beaten egg yolks. Season well with salt and pepper. Make into small balls around the size of a walnut and fry in a pan by rolling them around till they are brown all over.

Accompaniments to Game & Poultry

Boiled turkey or fowl — Boiled ham or bacon, melted butter, celery or parsley sauce

Roast turkey or fowl — Cranberry, chestnut or bread sauce, fried sausages

Duck or goose — Apple sauce, sage and onion stuffing

Wild duck — Orange sauce

Roast game — Bread sauce and fried bread crumbs

Jugged hare — Red-currant jelly

GARDINER'S Herbs

Tarragon
Artemisia dracunculus

COMMON NAME: mugwort, little dragon.

OCCURRENCE: cultivated in kitchen gardens across Europe and Great Britain. Tarragon originally arose from both Siberia and southern Europe to form the French and Russian tarragon we know today.

PARTS USED: the leaves, which contain an essential volatile oil which is lost on drying.

MEDICINAL USES: today there are few medicinal uses for tarragon but it has been used previously to stimulate the appetite and to cure toothache. Tarragon is mostly used in cooking-particularly on the European continent. It is used for dressings, salads, vinegar and pickles.

ADMINISTERED AS: fresh root, fresh herb.

Chicken Pie

a tarragon white sauce is lovely in the pie instead of the stock

I ken chickens are dear, but the way this pie is made, you'll get a pot o' soup and the next day's dinner out the bird too. Mind and cook the giblets too. The bird will stay juicy if simmered in the pot, not boiled. Keep any leftover stock for ither soups an' the leftover meat for the next day's tea.

1 medium-sized chicken	Forcemeat balls *see opposite page*
An onion	Slices of ham
White pepper and salt	3 hard-boiled eggs
1/2 teaspoon nutmeg	About 1/2 pint of stock
1/2 teaspoon mace	Rough puff pastry (see my recipe)

Put the chicken into a pot of water, add the onion and seasoning and simmer as you would for Cock-a-leekie soup. Simmer till the meat falls from the bone and strain, saving the lovely stock. Remove all the flesh from the bones. You can boil the bones and skin again to make more stock. Put a layer of chicken at the bottom of a pie-dish, then a layer of ham, then forcemeat balls and hard-boiled eggs, cut in rings. Season each layer. Fill the dish and pour in stock to cover. Cover with rough puff pastry and mak' a hole in the middle. Bake in a moderate oven for 1 1/2 tae 2 hours.

59

BOILED TURKEY

This is a good way to keep an older turkey moist. Put into seasoned boiling water in a very big pot, with chopped onion and celery. Simmer for 1 ½ hours, or more, till the flesh comes away from the bone. Serve with vegetables and bread sauce made from the stock. Cool, skim off the fat and use for roasting potatoes and use the remaining stock for soup.

Stewed Duck

1 Duck, whole
2 Onions, chopped
Beef Dripping
Sage and Thyme, chopped
Pepper and Salt
Beef stock
Butter
Flour

Brown the duck in dripping in a pot. Then add onions and sauté for 20 minutes till soft. Pour out the dripping from the pot, and pour in enough beef stock to cover duck. Add chopped herbs and simmer till tender (about 1 hour, test with a knife). Slice the duck. Strain gravy and thicken with a little butter and flour. Bring to boil. Serve with potatoes and fresh green peas.

ROAST TURKEY

Forcemeat
1 pint of Stock made from Giblets
¼ lb. fat Bacon
½ oz. Flour
Salt
Pepper

Prepare and dress turkey, fill the loose skin of the breast with forcemeat, skewer down and cover with fat bacon or greased paper. Roast slowly, allowing 10 or 12 minutes to the pound. About ½ hour before it is done, remove the bacon or paper and return to the oven. When done, pour the fat and juice from the tin. Separate the fat from the juice. To the juice add the flour and the stock made from giblets and some seasoning. Boil up, add browning if necessary, and strain. Serve turkey with roast potatoes and with bread sauce.

Roast Chicken

Mind an keep the giblets and bones frae the bird for stock making. Also mind that a stuffed bird takes longer tae cook. You can cook some stuffing separately if you cook it in a covered oven dish. Give a chicken 20 minutes per pound in a hot oven, and another 20 minutes for good measure.

A wee chicken (about 2lb)

Stuffing: 3 oz. breid crumbs, 2 oz. suet, a few leaves of parsley (chopped), pepper and salt, and 1 egg

Prepare the chicken, tak' oot the giblets — or get the butcher tae dae it, but mind and ask for them. Wash the chicken and coat a' ower in butter. Mak' the stuffing. Draw up the legs under the wings and stuff the chicken's breast. Place a buttered paper ower the birdie, and baste frequently. Roast in a hot oven for at least 1 hour. Pierce the flesh and if the juice runs clear it is cooked. If not, cook for longer. Serve wi' guid, clear gravy, roast tatties and breid sauce.

recipe for bread sauce on page 12

61

Boiling Meat

Aims:
1. To retain the nourishment.
2. To serve tender, juicy meat.

Rules:
1. Put into boiling salted water.
2. Boil quickly 5 minutes, then simmer.

Average Times:
Beef — 15 mins. to each lb. and 15 mins. over.
Mutton — 20 mins. to each lb. and 20 mins. over
Pork — 25 mins. to each lb. and 25 mins. over.
Salt Meat — 30 mins. to each lb. and 30 mins. over

Suitable Cuts:
Beef — Round brisket
Mutton — Shoulder, leg

Roasting Meat

Moderate oven, 350°F, 180°C, gas mark 4 to 5:

Chicken	20 minutes per lb (45 per kg) plus 20 minutes
Beef Rare	20 minutes per lb (45 per kg) plus 20 minutes
Beef Medium	25 minutes per lb (55 per kg) plus 20 minutes
Beef Well-done	30 minutes per lb (66 per kg) plus 30 mins
Pork Medium	30 minutes per lb (66 per kg) plus 30 minutes
Pork Well-done	35 minutes per lb (77 per kg) plus 35 minutes
Lamb Medium	25 minutes per lb (55 per kg) plus 25 mins at 350°F
Lamb Well-done	30 minutes per lb (66 per kg) plus 30 mins at 350°F
Mutton	40-45 minutes per lb (88 to 99 per kg) at 350°F
or	First 15 minutes at 500°F (250°C) then 25-30 minutes per lb (55-66 per kg) at 350°F
Venison	15-20 minutes per lb (33-44 per kg)

Meat

Important things tae mind when cooking meats, are:— buy it from a guid butcher, pay attention to yer cooking times, temperature, seasoning, and mak' sure it is basted enough so it disna dry oot. Butcher meat is dear, so you dinna want to be spoiling it by doing anything ower fancy tae it either, in my opinion.

63

Cold Roast Beef

Beef should be cut in slices, the gravy brought to the boil and the slices cooked in it just long enough to heat through. Stewing toughens it, unless gently simmered 1 hour.

Steamed Beef

4 lb. of lean beef
Bacon
3 large onions
salt

Cut some thin strips of bacon and with a sharp-pointed knife make small holes in the steak and stick the bacon into the beef. Cut up three large onions and lay them in a bowl. Rub a little salt over the beef and lay it on the onions. Place the bowl in pan of boiling water and steam for 4 hours. When served, the meat will be very tender and there will be plenty o' guid, rich gravy.

CUTS OF BEEF

Hindquarter:
Hough or knuckle— Soups, stews, etc.
Rump (or round), silverside— Steaks, beef-ham, boiling, spicing and pickling
Pope's-eye— Grilling
Fillet— Grilling
Flank— Boiling
"Nine holes"— Boiling
Sirloin— Roasting (English cut)

Forequarter:
Hough or knuckle— Soups, stews, etc.
Runner, thick end— Stewing
Shoulder— Stewing Steaks, pie meat, etc.
Head— Cheek, tongue, palate

CUTS OF VEAL

Fed Veal:
Gigot— Roast or cutlets
Loin— Roast or cutlets
Shoulder— Stew, or stuffed, etc.
Runner— Stew
Breast— Stew
Knuckle— Soup
Head— Mock turtle soup
Feet— Jelly
Immature veal "Slink"— Only fit for boiling or stewing

Roast Beef

I have tae admit it's no' often we can afford a nice bit o' silverside, so I always cook it quite plain, and coat it in plenty o' butter to keep it juicy. Ye'll hae braw gravy if ye dredge the beef wi' flour when half cooked.

Cook it in a hot oven wi' 1/4 hour tae each lb. Heat the roasting tin in the oven and, when hot, pit your beef on a rack in the tin. Put some water in the oven tae keep it moist. Tae dish, lift the meat fae the tin, pour aff the fat, leaving the sediment in the tin. Add tae it a cupful of strong beef stock or gravy. Stir in a pan ower the heat till boiling.

Accompaniments to Meat

Boiled Beef — carrot and turnip.

Boiled Salt Beef — dumplings, green vegetable.

Boiled Mutton — Carrot and turnip. Caper Sauce.

Fried Steak — Chips. parsley butter.

Roast Beef — Yorkshire Pudding, gravy, Roast Potatoes.

Roast Lamb — Mint Sauce, gravy.

Roast Mutton — Red-currant Jelly, gravy.

Roast Pork — Apple Sauce, gravy.

Roast Venison — Red-currant Jelly, gravy.

Sirloin and ribs of beef — Horse-radish sauce and Yorkshire pudding, or tomato sauce; pickles

Hot ox tongue — Red-currant jelly

Grilled steak — Pickled walnuts or oyster sauce

Tripe — Onion sauce

Roast leg or saddle of mutton — Red-currant jelly

Boiled leg or neck of mutton — Caper sauce

Roast shoulder of mutton — Onion sauce

Mutton cutlets — Tomato sauce

Sheep's or calf's head — Parsley sauce

Roast lamb — Mint sauce

Roast pork — Apple sauce and forcemeat balls

Roast veal — Tomato, mushroom, onion or cranberry sauce, Horse-radish and lemons are good

Devilled Beef

Some slices of cold roast beef
1 tbsp of mustard
Pinch of salt
Worcestershire sauce
Cup of water
Gravy

Mix the mustard, salt, water, a splash of Worcestershire sauce to a cream; spread over the beef. Place in frying pan with some strong gravy poured round the base. Reheat the beef and serve with vegetables.

Devilled beef
bye The Twins

Take call'd Roast
beef Frae The
Larder before maw
adds ony Thing
Like The abuv Tae iT.
PUT iT in a piece.
EaT.
Reapeat Till There's
nane LefT.

Fillet of Beef A La Creme

Get a fillet of roasting beef; remove fat and skin. Sprinkle over pepper and a little salt. Skewer it into nice shape and lard it with fat bacon. Place it on baking-tin; place a large piece of butter over meat and cook it slowly in the oven, basting frequently. (1/2 lb. beef takes half-an-hour to cook.) When ready, pour off fat, and pour round beef 1 gill cream. Place tin on slow heat to heat cream thoroughly and baste meat with it. Place meat on dish with cream round it. Cream will be a pale brownish colour, because of the fat which adhered to tin, and because of basting meat.

Fillet of Beef

This is a dear cut o' beef. It shouldna be cooked ower much, but still be a wee bit pink in the middle. This is how they cooked it in the Big Hoose where me and Betty worked. This is no' how Betty likes it though. She likes hers burnt tae a crisp, the traditional way, but tae me that's a waste. Cut some fillets o' beef into rounds that are 1 inch thick and 2 1/2 inches wide. Beat them slightly flatter. Sprinkle wi' pepper and salt and fry in a hot pan, not turning too often. A piece o' fat under and above each round fillet keeps it juicy. (To test it, press the meat with your finger after about 4 minutes each side – there should still be a bit o' spring in it.)

Fillet of Beef with Mushroom

Cook as above. When cooked, place them on rounds of fried tomato, and on top of each fillet put a large fried mushroom, with a ball of butter in the centre of each mushroom. Serve this with spinach and tatties.

Boiled Brisket

2 lb. brisket

Salt

Carrot and turnip

1 onion

Boiling water

Plunge the meat into boiling, salted water and boil it quickly for 5 minutes, then simmer it for 1 hour. Add vegetables, chopped, 45 minutes before serving. This is lovely hot with vegetables or cold on sandwiches wi' pickle. Keep the stock for soups or sauces.

ROAST LEG OF LAMB

1 2.2-kg/5-lb leg of lamb
Butter
Sea salt
6 sprigs of fresh rosemary
Lamb stock
Balsamic vinegar
Red wine

6 large floury potatoes
4 large parnips (really, just as many as you think you will all eat)

Rub the meat all over a with a generous quantity of butter and place on a roasting pan. Sprinkle with a little sea salt. Chop half of the rosemary roughly and sprinkle over the butter-covered joint, then snap the remainder into little sprigs that can be shoved into the flesh of the lamb. Roast for twenty minutes in an oven preheated to 220°C/425°F/ gas mark 7. While the lamb is roasting, prepare the roast potatoes and parsnips. Cut the potatoes into quarters, and the parsnips lengthways into fingers, and parboil for around 10 to 15 minutes. Baste in oil and cover in ground sea salt and chopped rosemary and roast till they are golden brown. Reduce the heat to 190°C/375°F/gas mark 5 and roast for a further hour. Remove the lamb from the roasting pan and leave it to rest for around 20 to 30 minutes. Move the pan to the top of the stove in order to make a gravy. Turn on a low heat and heat the pan. Add a generous splash of good balsamic vinegar to the pan and mix with the lamb juices with a wooden spoon. Add about half a glass of red wine and reduce. Taste the gravy and season as necessary. Serve with the roast vegetables and boiled sugar-snap peas.
Serves four to six (with leftovers).

tattie fritters and
onion rings are guid
wi' this, Maw!

Fried Steak

1/2 lb. pope's eye steak, 3/4 inch thick

Suet fat

A guid dod o' butter

Get frying pan guid an' hot. Rub it with a bit o' suet fat.
Melt some butter an' dip the steak into it on baith sides.
Cook over a guid heat. Gie it 1 minute tae each side; this
seals it. Turn heat down and cook for 4 minutes each side,
remove frae heat and rest the meat. It's ready when it's a
braw broon colour.

Savoury Fritters

5 oz. Onions
1 tsp powdered Sage
4 Eggs
4 oz. Stale Bread

Soak bread thoroughly for 1 hour in a little
boiling water and covered over ; then mash with
fork, picking out hard pieces. Boil the onion till
quite soft ; chop it small ; add the sage, pepper
and salt and the eggs well beaten. Mix the whole
well with the bread and fry in fritters about 1/2
inch thick and 3 inches broad.

Steamed Steak

1 1/2 lb. steak
Onion, minced small
Flour
Pepper and salt

Cut the steak into nice pieces for rolling up,
dip each piece in the flour, pepper and salt, and
on each bit of steak put a little of the minced
onion, and roll up. Lay the pieces in a basin,
add a tablespoonful of water or stock and a little
ketchup or gravy powder. Cover the basin with
greased paper. Steam for 2 1/2 hours.

Steamed Mutton

Put the meat into a basin and put the basin into a saucepan with enough boiling water to reach half-way up. Add pepper and salt to the meat and allow 1/2 hour to each lb. When cooked, it will be beautifully tender. Serve with the gravy from the pot mixed with chopped capers.

Breast of Mutton

Take out the bones and fat. For the stuffing: take 6 tablespoonfuls grated bread, 1 dessertspoon parsley, 1 teaspoon mixed herbs, 1 small chopped onion, 1/2 teaspoon salt, 1/4 dessertspoon pepper, 1 egg and a little milk. Roll up the mutton after spreading this mixture over. Tie with string. Brown in a pan with a little dripping; add 1 onion and a cup of water. Stew for 1 1/2 hours.

CUTS OF MUTTON

Gigot — Roasting and chops
Loin — Chops or roast
Flank — Boiling
Breast — Boiling
Runner — Boiling
Shoulder — Roasting
Neck — Boiling, stewing, broth, etc.

mint

70

Mint sauce is on page 151

Roast Shoulder o' Mutton

Mutton needs slow cooking, Maggie, to make it tender. Cook 15 minutes in a hot oven then 40 minutes tae each lb. in a moderate oven.

Stuffing:

Cup of breid crumbs

1/2 cup suet

1 tablespoon parsley

Mixed herbs

Grated rind of lemon and the juice

1/2 teaspoon salt

Pepper, less than 1/2 teaspoon

Yolk of egg

Place a' the dry ingredients in a small basin and add lemon juice and egg. Wipe the mutton, take out the bones and spread the stuffing over it. Tie it up, and untie once cooked. The oven should be very hot. Place in the oven on a dish within a tin filled wi' water. After 15 minutes, reduce heat to moderate. Pour dripping over the roast and baste frequently. Untie. Serve with mint sauce, peas and new potatoes.

Lamb Hot Pot

2 mutton chops
1 sheep's kidney
1 onion
Tatties cut in thin
slices
1 small spoonful
Worcestershire sauce
A tbsp dripping or
butter
Salt and pepper

Put a layer of the
chopped tatties in
the bottom of a deep
oven dish. Then a
layer of chops and
kidney cut in pieces.
Fill up with tatties
and onion cut in
pieces, with sauce
and a little water.
Cover with greased
paper ; put in the
oven for 1 1/2 hours.

GARNISHING MEAT, POULTRY, ETC.

Roast beef may have small heaps of grated horse-radish placed round the dish, or Yorkshire pudding cut in squares.

Cold roast beef, if cut in slices, has a pretty border of beetroot and lemon in alternate slices, with a tiny sprig of parsley on the beetroot and a small diamond cut out of beetroot on each slice of lemon.

Cold boiled beef is decorated with boiled carrots cut in slices, triangles, squares or strips.

Cold roast mutton may be adorned with pickled eggs cut in half, each half placed cut side up and a sprig of green parsley placed on it. Sometimes the garnish is of parsley jelly, sometimes of lettuce.

Cold boiled mutton.—Turnip and carrot cut in fancy shapes garnish this dish, with a small heap of pickled nasturtium seeds placed at equal distances.

Game is garnished with barberries, red-currant jelly, or rowan jelly.

Poultry, rabbit, etc., are made attractive with a few slices of lemon with a tiny sprig of parsley on each.

CUTS OF PORK

Flank — Rolled for boiling, or simply cut for the same
Breast — Streaky bacon
Shoulder — Roast
Loin — Roast
Neck — Sliced bacon
Runner — Sliced bacon
Gigot — Roast
Shanks — Boiling, potted meat, etc.
Head — "Hungry John," Bath chops

Roast Pork

Allow 30 minutes tae the pound, in a moderate oven. Dinna ever undercook pork. The loin, ham and shoulder are the joints generally roasted. The pork should be young and the skin finely scored. Rub salt and butter over the skin and roast. Serve with apple sauce and butter beans.

Pork Chops

4 good sized pork chops
2 cooking apples, sugar

Slice the apples and stew with enough sugar to sweeten to taste. Place the pork chops under a hot grill, cook each side thoroughly. Cover with apple sauce and place under grill to caramelise the apple sauce. Serves two.

Irish Stew

1 lb. Neck of Mutton
8–10 Potatoes
2 onions
Salt and pepper
1/2 pt. water or stock

Chop and wash the meat, then slice the onions and potatoes. Arrange alternate layers of meat, onions, and potatoes in a pot. Season, and add water, simmer, and bring slowly to boil. Simmer gently 1 hour. Pile up on a hot ashet.
Is this no' just Stovies?

MACDUFF'S
N° 11
SCOTTISH FOODS OF QUALITY

Pork Cutlets

Ingredients: 1½ ozs. suet
2 apples
Salt
Pepper
6 pork cutlets
1½ ozs. butter
Brown gravy
Onions

METHOD: Take some cutlets and trim them neatly. Season with salt and pepper, and place them on a hot gridiron, greased with suet, over a clear fire or under a grill. Cook for ¼ hour or 20 minutes, turning several times. Arrange on a hot dish, and pour round brown gravy. Garnish with braised onions and quarters of apples fried lightly in a little suet.

PRIORITY

POST OFFICE TELEGRAM

Charges to pay

...... s ......

RECEIVE
PM 11

No. 38R
OFFICE STAMP

CONFIRM
SHE....
21-....

	Prefix	Time handed in	Office of origin and service instructions	Words	
GW S	43	134 12.18 FI/T OHMS 68			To.

From

PRIORITY-CC   MAW BROON 10 GLEBE STREET

SCOTLAND

ON LEAVE + STOP + HOME MONDAY + STOP +

FOR TWO WEEKS AUGUST + STOP +

MAKE MINCE AND TATTIES AND DUMPLING + STOP +

JOE

For free repetition of doubtful words telephone "TELEGRAMS ENQUIRY" or call with this form A or C
at office of delivery. Other enquiries should be accompanied by this form, and, if possible, the envelope.

An' they were were
jist BRAW!
Thanks, Maw,
love Joe

74

Pies & Savoury Things

I've gathered a' my favourites here Maggie.
Ye'll need pastry recipes for a lot of them
and I'll include them later on.

GARDINER'S
Herbs
Onion
Allium cepa

OCCURRENCE:
originally native to south-west Asia and now cultivated around the globe.

PARTS USED:
the bulb.

MEDICINAL USES:
diuretic, expectorant, antiseptic. Although onions are extensively used in cookery, they also have medicinal uses. A roasted onion is applied to tumours or earache to remove the pain and onions steeped in gin produce a fluid extract which is given for gravel and dropsy. A homeopathic remedy is made from red onions and is useful in neuralgic pain, colds, hay fever, toothache and in the early stages of laryngitis with hoarseness.

ADMINISTERED AS: poultice, tincture.

Sausage Rolls

8 ozs. rough puff pastry
1/4 teaspoon salt
8 oz. sausages
cold water

Blanch sausages and skin them. Cut pastry into pieces five inches square. Place 1/2 sausage on each, wet edges, turn over, and press edges. Trim edges. Brush over with egg and cook in a hot oven for 20 to 30 minutes.

rough puff pastry is on page 129

Nº 14

MACDUFF'S

SCOTTISH FOODS OF QUALITY

Ingredients: 3/4 lb. short pastry   1/2 lb. sausage
1 egg   Parsley

METHOD: If sausages are used, remove the skin, but these rolls may be made from sausage meat bought from the butcher. Roll out the pastry, and cut into oblong pieces. Lay a piece of sausage meat in the centre of each piece of pastry. Wet round the edges and double the pastry over. Put the rolls on to a greased baking tin, brush them over with a slightly beaten yoke of an egg, and bake them in a good oven until nicely browned and well cooked.

Sausage Rolls

Beef Olives

1 lb. steak
1 oz. dripping
Salt and pepper
3/4 pt. water
1 oz. flour
Carrot and turnip
  Stuffing:
2 oz. bread crumbs
1 teasp. chopped parsley
1 oz. chopped suet
Salt and pepper
Milk to bind

MIX stuffing into a stiff paste. Cut steak into strips 2 in. wide, put 1 teasp. mixture on each, roll up and tie with string. Brown well in hot fat, pour off surplus fat. Add boiling water and simmer 3/4 hour. Add sliced vegetables and cook 3/4 hour or until tender. Remove string from olives, season, and thicken gravy. Serve neatly on a hot ashet.

Steak and Kidney Pie

1/2 lb. rough puff pastry

1 sheep's kidney

1 lb. thinly cut steak

Water

Seasoned flour

YOU WOOD HARDLY COOK in a cold oven, wood you?

Cook in a hot oven. Cut steak intae neat strips, trim and wash kidney. Dip a' the meat in seasoned flour; wrap a piece of kidney and suet in each strip of meat. Fill pie-dish and add water. Roll out the pastry a little larger than the pie-dish, cut aff a strip a' round and place on the wetted edge of pie-dish. Cover the pie with strips or patterns made frae the remaining pastry if you like. Trim and mark wi'' a knife. Make a hole in centre. Brush with beaten egg and bake in hot oven till pastry is cooked, then in moderate oven until meat is cooked (1 1/2 tae 2 hours). Add a wee drap o' hot stock, through the hole in the top, if it's needed, and serve from the ashet on the table.

77

Hot water pastry

8 oz lard or dripping
1 1/2 lb self-raising flour
1 teaspoon salt
10 fl oz water
Milk for glazing

In a saucepan, melt the lard in the boiling water. Sieve the flour into a bowl that has been warmed (so that your hot fat and water mixture is not chilled by the flour). Make a well in the middle of the flour and mix in the hot fat and water mixture with a wooden spoon. Once the mixture has cooled a little, knead the dough. When the dough is elastic, leave it in a warm place until it becomes firmer yet still elastic enough to roll out.

Veal and Ham Pie

Rough puff pastry
1 lb. of veal
1/4 lb. ham
1 hard-boiled egg, sliced
1/2 tsp herbs
1/8 pint stock
1/2 tsp salt
1/4 tsp pepper
1 tsp chopped parsley
Grated lemon rind

Cut the ham into small pieces. Chop the parsley and mix the seasonings together. Cut the veal into pieces 2 inches long, and dip into the seasonings. Place a layer of veal at the bottom of the pie-dish, then, place a layer of bacon on top. When dish is half filled, pour in the stock and a layer of sliced boiled egg. Fill the dish with the rest of the ham and veal. Cover with pastry. Make a hole in centre and bake in hot oven till the pastry turns brown then reduce heat to low and cook for 2 hours.

And mushy marrowfat peas an vinegar, Man, don't forget them

oh aye, Hen, dinna forget the mushy peas ... an' chips tae!

Scotch Pies

This is footery, I'll no' pretend it isnae. But ye just canny tell whit some butchers put in their mutton pies, so it's nice to mak' yer ain for a change.

Hot water pastry   see the recipe opposite
1 lb finely minced beef or lamb
8 oz finely crushed rusks or fine breid crumbs
Seasoning of salt, white pepper, and mace or nutmeg

Whit would the Volunteer Arms dae withoot them?

Roll out the pastry till it is about ⅛ inch thick. Cut out rounds that will fit whichever moulds you're using — the pastry should make around 15 pies or more. Cut out enough circles fae the pastry tae make tops for the pies.

Mix the mince with the rusk or breid crumbs. Add water or gravy and bind together, then add the seasoning and mix thoroughly. Fill the pie shells three quarters full, add the tops and seal. Make slits, or wee circles, in the pie tops tae let the steam out and brush with milk. Preheat the oven tae high. Bake for 25 minutes or until golden broon.

79

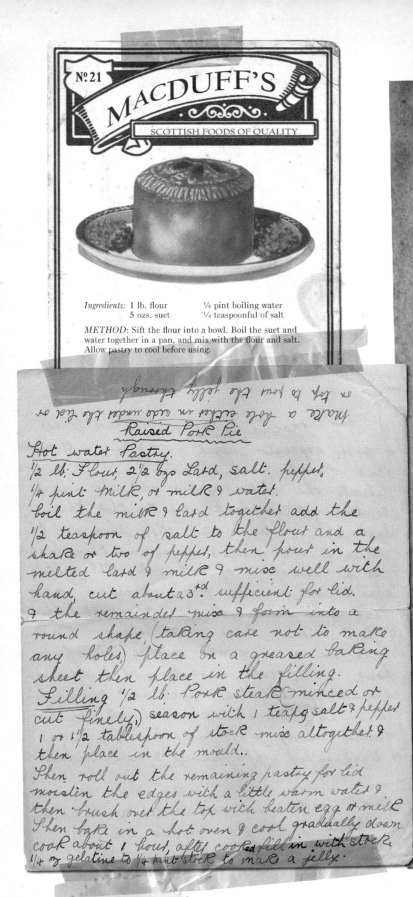

MACDUFF'S

Nº 21

SCOTTISH FOODS OF QUALITY

Ingredients: 1 lb. flour   ¼ pint boiling water
5 ozs. suet   ¼ teaspoonful of salt

METHOD: Sift the flour into a bowl. Boil the suet and water together in a pan, and mix with the flour and salt. Allow pastry to cool before using.

Raised Pork Pie

Hot water Pastry.
½ lb. Flour, 2½ ozs Lard, salt. pepper.
¼ pint Milk, or milk & water.
boil the milk & lard together add the
½ teaspoon of salt to the flour and a
shake or two of pepper, then pour in the
melted lard & milk & mix well with
hand, cut about a 3rd sufficient for lid,
& the remainder mix & form into a
round shape (taking care not to make
any holes) place on a greased baking
sheet then place in the filling.
Filling ½ lb. Pork steak (minced or
cut finely,) season with 1 teaspg salt & pepper
1 or 1½ tablespoon of stock mix altogether &
then place in the mould..
Then roll out the remaining pastry for lid
moisten the edges with a little warm water &
then brush over the top with beaten egg or milk
Then bake in a hot oven & cool gradually down
cook about 1 hour, after cooked fill in with stock.
¼ oz gelatine to ¼ pint stock to make a jelly.

Make a hole either in side under the lid or
a top to pour the jelly through.

Leek Pie

10 leeks, chopped
        finely

Short crust pastry
1¼ pint milk
1 beaten egg
Salt
Pepper
Butter

Wash leeks and
fry in butter for
20 minutes. Then
simmer in 4 tbsps
milk. Put into a pie
dish with about a
1¼ pint of milk and
a beaten egg. Add
salt, pepper and
butter.
    Cover with
pastry and bake for
about 1½ hour.

Hogmanay Steak Pie

2lb stewing steak

1 tablespoon seasoned plain flour

2oz dripping

1 large onion, chopped

3 large carrots

1 pint beef stock

Worcestershire sauce

9 oz puff pastry

Toss the steak in the seasoned flour. Melt the dripping in a large saucepan and brown the meat, and them remove and put aside. Fry the onions and the carrots until softened slightly and then return the meat tae the pan. Add a couple of dashes o' Worcestershire sauce, black pepper and salt tae the beef stock, and pour into the pan. Cover and bring tae the boil, then reduce the heat and simmer, still covered, for twa hours, checking noo and again. (If ye're busy ye can put it aside tae cool, have a wee new year dram, and mak' the pie the next day!) Pour the stew into a 3-pint ashet. Roll out the pastry and press down firmly around the sides of the ashet and on top of the stew. Brush the top wi" beaten egg or some milk and score into criss-crosses. Mak' a hole in the centre tae let the steam oot. Cook for 30 minutes in the centre o' a hot oven.

Clapshot is Orcadian, that is, from Orkney.

Stop showing aff, Horace, we a' ken ye're brainy.

Clapshot
from Mrs Frame

1 lb floury tatties, boiled
1 lb turnip, chopped and boiled
1 onion, fried
2 tbsps chopped chives
Salt and pepper
3 oz butter

Boil the tatties and turnip. Gently fry the chopped onions in 25 g/1 oz butter until soft but not brown. Mash the boiled potato and boiled turnip together with the remaining butter and the fried onions. Once mashed, mix in the chopped chives and the seasoning. Serve hot with oatcakes or as an accompaniment to haggis. ——

Cold-Beef and Tomato Pie

4 small Tomatoes

1/2 lb. cold Boiled Beef

1 Egg

Parsley

Pepper

1/2 gill beef gravy — make by adding 1 teaspoon of Bisto to a cup of water

Cut tomatoes into slices, and beef into neat, small pieces, removing skin and gristle. Arrange in alternate layers and pour over beaten egg, mixed wi' stock, like custard (no' too full). Dish is lined round sides with pastry, edges being well covered, and strips of paste arranged diagonally over top. Then cover edge richt roon' and mark neatly. Glaze wi' egg or milk and bake 3/4 hour.

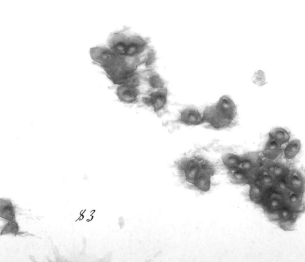

PROGRESSIVE WHIST.

Name...... A. Clough

Table No.	No. of Deal	Tricks Scored	Total	Signature
	1	7	7	m.Q. 50

White or Mealie Pudding

2 lbs. oatmeal toasted
1 lb. beef suet
2 onions, finely chopped and fried
Salt
Pepper
1 tsp sugar
Tripe skins, scalded

Fry the onions. Toast the oatmeal on a baking tray in the oven. Combine the suet with the onions, and then mix with the toasted oatmeal. Add the salt, pepper, and sugar. Mix thoroughly and put the mixture in the prepared tripe skins. The mixture will swell so leave a little room within the skins for this. Tie the ends. Drop the puddings into boiling water. Prick with a fork to prevent them bursting. Cook for an hour. The puddings will keep for some time if kept chilled and dry. When needed reheat in hot dripping.

Skirlie

Skirlie is a guid accompaniment tae game dishes and is also braw as a stuffing for meat. I could eat a plate o' it itsel'!

2 oz butter or dripping
1 onion, chopped
3 1/2 oz medium or coarse oatmeal
Salt and pepper

Melt the butter or dripping in a frying pan and fry the onion until soft but no' ower crispy. Then add the oatmeal gradually and gie it a richt guid stir till a' the fat sooks in. Serve hot as an accompaniment tae meats or it can be left tae cool and used as a stuffing for roasts. Yer faither-in-law likes it cauld, wi' ane or twa pickled eggs! Pickled eggs indeed — if he hudnae married me I'd say he had nae taste at a'.

85

Ham and Steak Roll

¾ **lb rump steak**
¼ **lb Ayrshire bacon (middle)**
1 egg
Breadcrumbs made from 1 to 2
slices plain bread
Worcestershire sauce (optional)
Black pepper

Mince together the steak and ham. You can ask your butcher to do this if you do not have a mincer. Mix with the egg and breadcrumbs and add a couple of dashes of Worcestershire sauce (if you like it) and some ground black pepper.

Place in a pudding basin and cover with greaseproof paper that is folded into a pleat in the middle to allow the air in the jar to expand but not escape, and tie with string. Place in a large pot filled with boiling water and steam for two hours.

Place a weight on top of the meat roll once it is cooked and leave overnight. This is to make sure that it is firm enough for slicing. Loosen the roll from the jar with a pallet knife.

Can be served hot with green vegetables and boiled potatoes or cold with salad.

It is especially nice as a cold sandwich filling with pickle or chutney.

TONGUE

To Boil a Tongue

Tie up firmly in a good shape. Place in boiling water with 2 carrots, 1 turnip, 1 onion, 1 bunch herbs, 12 peppercorns, 1 blade mace.

Simmer gently 3 hours. Take out and skin tongue while hot. Press meat between two boards. Put tongue in press, cake tin or basin with board on top and a weight. Leave till cold. Melt two leaves of gelatine in cup of liquor and pour over tongue or meat.

WORM LOAF
20 CHOPED WORMS
A PINT OF BEETLE JUICE
7LB SELF RAISIN FLOWER
4 BEATEN ANTS EGGS
5 GROUND UP SPIDER SKINS
7 OZ DRIED SLATERS
AN EARYWIG PER PERSON
A JENNY LONG LEGS TO GARNISH

MIX UP AN COOK IN MAW'S BEST LOAF TIN FOR 40 MINUTES IF SHE DOESN'T CATCH YOU FIRST. SERVES 9 FOWK. NO' ENOUGH LEFT FOR US. OH DEAR. SMELLS BOGGIN, LOOKS BOGGIN, AND BY GOLLY IT IS BOGGIN, BUT WE BET IT ISNAE AS BOGGIN AS BOILED TONGUE! GROOOOOOOOO!

86

SEE ALSO, FLY SEMETRIES

Forfar Bridies

No tae be confused wi Dundee 'pehs'

1 lb beef rump, roughly minced or chopped

3 oz grated beef suet

1 onion, finely grated or chopped

Suet pastry

Mind, Forfar bridies are horseshoe-shaped, they're not like Cornish pasties

Mince the beef. Grate the onion finely and mix wi' the beef an' suet. Roll out the pastry and divide it into fower pieces that are twice as long as they're broad. Place the filling on one half o' the pastry, lengthwise, and wet the edges wi' some water. Fold the remaining pastry over the top and press down firmly around the edges. Trim and mak' into horseshoe shapes and pinch the pastry around the edges. Mak' a wee slit in the top tae let the steam oot while the meat cooks. Let the bridies chill somewhere cool for half an hour tae let the pastry rest. Then place them on a greased baking tray and bake in an hot oven preheated for between 30 and 40 minutes. Serve hot, straight frae the oven. Maks fower.

Suet Pastry

12 oz plain flour
A pinch of salt
3 oz unsalted butter, diced
3 oz suet
Water

Sieve flour and salt into bowl. Add butter and suet. Rub together with fingers and bind with cold water. Mix to make firm dough. Rest dough for one hour.

Scotch Eggs

5 eggs
1 lb. pork sausagemeat
Breadcrumbs
Dripping

Hard boil four of the eggs, and beat up the fifth. Peel the boiled eggs. Divide the sausagemeat into four. Dip the hard-boiled eggs in beaten egg and mould the pork sausagemeat around them. Dip in more egg and then cover in breadcrumbs. Fry in deep fat for ten minutes. Perfect served cold with salad.

The eggs could also be coated with forcemeat. To your normal forcemeat recipe add chopped anchovy, capers, fried minced onions, mixed spice, and salt and pepper. Again, cover in breadcrumbs and deep fry.

Macaroni Cheese

1 cup macaroni
1 tablespoon butter
1 tablespoon flour
1 cup milk
½ cup grated cheese
½ teaspoon salt
½ teaspoon white pepper
1 boiled egg, chopped (optional, but I like it)
1 cup toasted breadcrumbs
A wee bit more grated cheese for the top

Boil the macaroni in salted water — don't let it get soggy — till it's just cooked. Make a white sauce with the butter, flour and milk (I'll not insult you by telling you how to do this, Maggie). Add the cheese, salt and pepper, and the chopped, boiled egg. Throw the cooked macaroni into the sauce and pour it into an oven dish. Cover in toasted breadcrumbs and grated cheese and bake in a hot oven till golden brown on top. Easy!

Bacon and Egg Pie

This is Eleanor Purdie's recipe. You can really use whatever variations of the ingredients ye happen tae hae in yer larder. Which is guid if the gossipy Gows turn up unannounced expectin' their tea!

½ lb Ayrshire bacon

3 eggs

2 dessert apples

¼ lb grated cheese

3 tomatoes

Mustard

Rough-puff pastry
(see the recipe, page 125)

Trim aff excess fat and fry the Ayrshire bacon, then chop it intae strips. Scramble, or boil and chop, the eggs. Slice the apples and the tomatoes. Roll out enough pastry tae fit an 8-inch sandwich tin, base and topping. On the bottom layer of pastry, spread a wee drappie mustard, and on top of this place the slices of apple. On top of the apple slices place the bacon, then the eggs, the tomatoes and finally the quarter pound of grated cheese. Place the pastry top on the pie, crimp at the edges tae seal, brush wi' beaten egg and then score with criss-crosses. Place in the middle of a hot oven until risen and golden brown. Serves six with assorted vegetables.

Lorne Sausage

This recipe makes quite a few so it's probably best to slice and freeze in small portions for a later date.

900 g/2 lb minced beef
900 g/2 lbs minced pork
1 egg, beaten
3 cups breadcrumbs or crushed rusk
2 tsp salt
2 tsp white pepper
2 tsp nutmeg
2 tsp powdered dried coriander seed
Water

Mix the beef and pork mince together. Mix in the beaten egg and add enough breadcrumbs to make a firm mixture. Add the salt, pepper and spices and mix thoroughly. Add some water if the mixture is a little too firm. Form the sausage into a long cuboid shape. Place in the freezer for a short time but dinna allow to freeze. This is simply to solidify the mixture to allow it to become easier to slice cleanly.
If you are freezing them once they are sliced, cut squares of greased paper or cellophane and place between each sausage slice and place a few in each freezer bag. Fry each sausage until golden brown and crusty on each side and serve in a warm, buttered bap with fried onions.

best meal of the day!

The one that's served with

H.P. SAUCE

H.P. is a wonderful help to the ca... housewife who prides hers... making every meal, howeve... appetising, wholesome, and en...

The exquisitely rich, satisfying flavou... of H.P.—derived from Orienta... and spices blended with Pure Ma... Vinegar — makes cold meat, c... cheese, fish, and everything else so tempting.

SAUSAGE ROLLS

8 ozs. pastry, any kind
1/4 teaspoonful salt
8 oz. sausages
cold water

Blanch sausages and skin them. Cut pastry into pieces five inches square. Place 1/2 sausage on each, wet edges, turn over, and press edges. Trim edges. Brush over with egg and cook in a hot oven for 20 to 30 minutes.

Daphne, why on earth would ye make yer ain square sausage when the butcher does it?

Musselburgh Pie

I've heard tell o' folk eating oysters raw! Whit a carry on. Musselburgh pie is the best place for them. The oysters, not the folk, although ...

1 lb. steak

1 dozen oysters

1 oz. flour

Salt and pepper

1 pint stock

1/2 lb. rough puff pastry

To a pie dish, add a china funnel. Use a wooden mallet to beat the steak until it is very thin. Open the oysters with a short knife. Beard them and halve them. Cut the steak into strips. Wrap each oyster half in a strip of meat. Add salt and pepper to the flour, dip each roll in this and pack in the pie-dish. Add the stock and cover with the pastry. Bake in a moderate oven for 1 1/2 hours.

Vegetables

There's nuthin' quite like a bilin' o' new tatties straight frae yer faither-in-law's allotment, or a pea pod straight aff the plant, or a fresh biled sprout dripping in butter. When ye have a faimily, mak' sure yer weans get vegetables for every meal, nae nonsense. If ye feed them wi' different anes as often as you can they'll no' be fussy eaters. I cannae abide fussy eaters. A little and often is my motto. Chips dinna count.

ON COOKING VEGETABLES
AND SOME VEGETARIAN DISHES

EVEN good cooking cannot improve poor or stale vegetables, so it is of great importance to buy fresh produce.

Do not soak green vegetables before they are to be washed, nor yet too long before you are to cook them.

If the greens appear to be rather wilted, after cutting and preparing, allow them 20 minutes in cold water without salt. This may revive them after which they can be placed in salted water and cooked in the ordinary way.

Soaking garden vegetables in salt will draw out the insects and slugs. Vegetables, such as cauliflower and Brussels sprouts, benefit from soaking in water with a little vinegar added, which draws out the insects more rapidly than salt. However, rinse them thoroughly before cooking.

Root vegetables should not be allowed to soak for a long time. The outsides should be well brushed and cleaned and the water discarded before peeling.

Steaming is better than boiling. Your food retains the goodness better. Root vegetables such as carrots and turnip are best steamed. A little salt should be sprinkled over them before cooking, and the water must be kept at boiling point.

Whether boiled or steamed, they are ready for serving when a knife may easily be thrust through them.

To keep a better colour when cooking green vegetables, do not place the lid on the saucepan. Root vegetables must always be covered for the steam improves them. For the more delicate vegetables such as peas and beans, a casserole and a minimum amount of water are to be recommended.

CABBAGE. Cabbages should be boiled till tender. Do not allow the water to boil too rapidly. This is the casue of the unpleasant odour that too often arises from cooking cabbage.

CAULIFLOWER. As with other vegetables take care not to overcook. Allow it to become just tender. If you want to cook a cauliflower very rapidly, then cut it into smaller pieces.

CARROTS. Always steam carrots. The small carrots have the more delicate flavour. Cut into circles before boiling or steaming because these taste sweeter than 'batons'.

PARSNIPS. Are best steamed, then mashed with butter or chopped into thin chips and roasted in dripping.

GREEN OR RUNNER BEANS. Trim the ends and pull, to strip away all stringy parts. Boil till tender.

MARROW OR COURGETTE. Try steaming or boiling a vegetable marrow in its jacket. Marrows and courgettes are delicious cooked in batter as fritters. Quick frying and crisp batter are a must. On the continent, marrow flowers are picked and fried in light batter and eaten as an aperitif.

MUSHROOMS. These may be gently stewed and served in the liquid, slightly thickened, or fried very gently in butter. Mushrooms are a lovely accompaniment to beef.

POTATOES. When potatoes are boiled in their jackets, they keep much more flavour. Scrub well before cooking of course. Choose floury potatoes for baking, mashing, chipping and roasting; and waxy potatoes for boiling.

PEAS. Peas are best steamed, sprinked with salt, wrapped in a lettuce or cabbage leaf.

BROAD BEANS. Only the smallest beans should be used. They should be shelled and boiled. Remove the skins of the beans before serving, coated butter.

SPINACH. Boil the spinach with a little soda and salt for 10 minutes. Press through a strainer, then rub through a wire sieve. Add two or three tablespoonfuls of cream, beating well.

Stoved Tatties

Stovies — withoot the meat!

Tatties
Butter
Salt
Water

Nº 15

MACDUFF'S

SCOTTISH FOODS OF QUALITY

METHOD: Wash, peel, and cut potatoes into long, thin pieces or into scallops. Dry in a clean cloth, and deep fry as follows. Sufficient suet should be put into deep frying pan to cover well the food to be fried. The temperature should then be raised until a piece of white bread dropped in turns golden-brown in half a minute. Tis temperature is reached without the appearance of any unpleasant fumes usually associated with frying.

Scalloped Potatoes

Peel the tatties, and put them over a low heat with just enough water tae cover the bottom of the pan. Add some salt and put wee dods of butter here and there. Cover and simmer gently till soft and melted. There should be no water left tae pour aff.

Dripping can be used instead o' butter but I prefer butter. Fried onions are nice to add, with plenty of pepper.

Champit Tatties with Sibies

8 medium potatoes (peeled)
Small bunch of spring onions
1/4 pt milk
Salt and pepper
A dod of butter per person

Boil the potatoes until they are soft. Drain and return them to the heat to dry slightly before mashing. Finely chop the white and green of the spring onions and cook in the milk. Beat this mixture into the mashed potatoes until they are fluffy and smooth. Season to taste and serve a generous helping onto each plate, topping with a dod of butter.

A 'recipe' for mashed tatties, Horace, oh how complicated! Did you invent that yersel?

Arran Potato Salad

10-12 cooked tatties, diced
1 cup green peas
1 cup diced pickled beetroot
Salt and pepper
1 tsp each of:
    Chopped chervil
    Chopped parsley
    Chopped shallot
Salad cream (enough to moisten)

Combine everything together. Easy!

Rumbledethumps

Is this no' a braw name?

1 lb potatoes

4 tablespoons single cream

1 lb cabbage, shredded

Salt and pepper

2 oz butter

1 tablespoon spring onions, chopped

1 tablespoon chives, chopped

1 small onion, chopped and fried

Bile the tatties for around 15 minutes. Shred the cabbage finely and boil until it is just cooked. This should take no more than 5 minutes. Fry the onion until brown and golden but no' too crispy. Mash the tatties till creamy and add the butter and cream. Mix well with the cabbage, chopped chives and fried onions. Season well with salt and pepper and taste it. Tip the ingredients into an ovenproof dish. At this point ye can put the dish aside tae be reheated later or ye can bake straight awa'. Ye could cover it wi'' grated cheese an a'. Bake for 30 minutes.

Macaroni and Tomatoes

Put 1/2 lb. macaroni in boiling water and boil it till just soft (test after 10 mins). Strain and put it in a baking-tin with pepper and salt to taste. Add the contents of a 2-lb. tin of tomatoes. Bake with a small piece of butter on top for 1/2 hour.

Very exotic cooking, Maw. NOT. None of your cheek, Daphne!

Vegetarian Haggis

1/2 lb. of flour
1/2 lb. of breadcrumbs
6 oz. of butter
A small onion chopped
A teacupful of pinhead oatmeal
1/2 cup of cooked lentils
2 Eggs
Vegetable stock

Melt butter, add to the dry ingredients and moisten with a little stock. Season with white pepper and a little salt to taste. Boil in a covered pudding basin for about 3 hours.

Vegetarian Pie

1 lb. potatoes
1/4 lb. mushrooms or tomatoes
1 large onion
1 oz. butter
Pepper and salt
Short pastry

Peel and slice potatoes, put in dish with mushrooms or tomatoes cut up, also onion and seasoning. On top put the butter broken up, add a little water. Cover with short pastry and bake 1 hour.

Potato Croquettes (right posh!)

1 lb. cooked tatties

1 oz. butter, melted

1 egg, beaten, and 1 yolk of an egg

Salt and pepper

Breid crumbs

Champ the tatties. Add the yolk o' an egg and the melted butter and a bit o' seasoning. Shape into croquettes (a kind of cylindrical shape). Coat with beaten egg and roll in breid crumbs. Fry in hot fat, or roast in hot oven if you're dieting, till golden brown.

Tattie Chips

Peel some tatties, and cut into chips. For extra crispiness, parboil the tatties first, then cool. Dry thoroughly. Fry in hot fat till broon. Drain, and season with salt. Serve with fried, battered haddock or — if my laddie has his way — everything!

Lang Kail

Ye might think the auld wummin has gone daft including a recipe for cooking cabbage. I know you're a good cook yersel Maggie, or gettin' that way, I'm only including it because I've been caught oot cooking kail (or kale) mysel'. Curly kail needs a lot o' cooking, more than white cabbage. My visitors were waiting and waiting on their denner and the kail was bubbling awa', still as tough as auld leather. The tatties were ready and waiting, turning grey, and my pie crust was burnt. I wis mortified. The older the leaf, the longer the cooking time, so pick young plants. I think it's best in broth, the goodness frae the leaves disna get thrown awa' wi' the water, but I do like the strong taste wi' meat.

Take twa or three stalks o' fresh crisp young green kail, separate the blades frae the stalk, wash well, shred it finely and boil till tender in salted water. This could take 20 minutes, but keep testing it. Drain and beat up the leaves wi' plenty o' butter, salt and pepper. Serve wi' pork or lamb.

BIRD'S CUSTARD

HOT

The Sauce Delicious!

We all know that children **love a treat**. Trust **the name of Bird's** to guarantee a delicious **warm surprise** for the **children** on those cold winter days.

Bird's Custard. Quality **food**.

So, pick up a pack with your shopping, today.

Available **in 1/2 lb and 1lb packs.**

...inter treat

CUSTARD SAUCE (PLAIN)

INGREDIENTS

1 *large teaspoonful Cornflour*
1 *Egg*
1 *teaspoonful Sugar*
1/2 *pint Milk*
Flavouring (if liked)

Blend the cornflour with a little **cold milk**. Heat **the** remainder of the milk.

Pour **over** the blended cornflour and return to pan. Stir till boiling, and cook thoroughly.

When sufficiently **cool**, pour over **the well-beaten** egg. Return to **the pan**, and stir over the **fire until the egg** is cooked, but do not boil.

Add sugar and flavouring. Serve hot or cold.

...spoonful castor sugar, 1 egg white, some glacé cherries and angelica.

Dissolve the jellies separately. Cut the cake into thin slices and spread with a little raspberry jam. Arrange them neatly at the bottom of a glass dish. Pour the raspberry jelly over and leave to set. Beat the egg white with the castor sugar, and when the lemon jelly is nearly cold beat the egg white and sugar into it, beating until the mixture looks like snow. Spread it over the top of the trifle.

Cut one long strip of angelica and put it in the middle of the snow. Cut six short strips, arrange these each side of the long strip to look like branches, then cut leaf shapes out of angelica and place them against the branches. Cut the cherries in halves and place them close to the stem to look like holly.

Mince pies

THIS is my Christmas fare masterpiece.—Mrs Janet Brown, 1 Burnbank Terrace, Thornton, Fife.

Mincemeat—6 oz. shredded suet, 6 oz. raisins, 6 oz. currants, 6 oz. sultanas, 4 oz. sugar, 1 oz. mixed peel, rind and juice of 1 lemon, rind and juice of 1 orange, and pinch salt. Mix all together.

Flaky Pastry.—8 oz. flour, 3 oz. margarine, 3 oz. lard, pinch salt, ½ teaspoonful lemon juice, cold water to mix.

Mix fats together and chop into flour, add salt and lemon juice. Mix to elastic dough with water.

Cut pastry into circles. Put mincemeat in centre and cover with other circle. Cut two slits in top and sprinkle with castor sugar. Bake in hot oven till golden brown.

Custard party pieces

A CREAMY filling of pears, walnuts, and custard makes these iced pastry squares very nice.—Miss W. Martin, 34 Balgarvie Crescent, Cupar, Fife.

Cut ½ lb. of flaky pastry rolled out to ¼ in. thickness into 2-in. squares and bake in a hot oven for

...to the boil and pour over blended mixture, stirring all time.

Return all to the pan and b... 3 minutes. Cut the pears into pieces and add to the custard chopped walnuts. Allow to c...

With a sharp knife split flaky square and fill with mixture. Mix two tablesp... icing sugar with a little hot... to a smooth cream. Place icing on to top of each squa... smooth with a wet knife.

A half walnut can be pl... the centre of the icing as ...tion.

●●●●●●●●●●●●●●●●●●●

SURPRISE

"BUT I've got one t... Jane presented Christmas.

Most mothers hav... and many of us are th... instead of delivering it...

It's a hard job to ...

I find the safest... tiny soldiers and an... present your gifts in a...

The giant crack... separately then tie th... parcel in red crepe ... centre. Gather the cr... to form a cracker. A... finishing touch.

It is an easy m... idea with the aid of ... a simple little three... top, "Johnny's Gara...

It does mean a... but that, I feel, is... Mrs R. C. Paulin, 1...

●●●●●●●●●●●●●●●●

Meg Fraser

...and cacti together ...r two tiny figures, ...effect is decorative. ...ady have gardens of ...you will no doubt ...lid, that there are ...le "fellows" in ...screaming for more ...these into your ...r gift will cost

...ours went off ...sale to buy a ...SHE is pretty ...is a wispy wee ...ever been to an ...and was gey ...making his bids. ...ad, and eventually ...hissed at him, ..."Are you a man ...or a mouse— SQUEAK up!" Several folk sitting around overheard, and howls of laughter "drowned out" the auctioneer. WHO told me this story—they BOTH did, good sports that they are.

DILLY DITHER.

Puddings

Best kept for Sundays in my opinion,
but yer bairnies and yer man will
love them.

Lemon Meringue Pie

1 baked pie crust (I ken you have a nice recipe for short crust pastry frae yer mither-in-law)

1 $\frac{1}{4}$ cups sugar

$\frac{1}{2}$ cup flour

$\frac{1}{8}$ tsp salt

1 cup boiling water

Grated rind of 1 lemon

3 eggs, separated (keep yolks and whites)

1 tbsp butter

4 $\frac{1}{2}$ tbsps lemon juice

$\frac{1}{2}$ cup castor sugar

Make the pie crust first. Then make the lemon curd. Mix sugar, flour and salt in a pot, add the cup of boiling water, stirring constantly. Allow it to come to boil, then take off stove and cook in double boiler for 15 minutes. Add butter, yolks, lemon juice and rind and mix well. Pour into the baked pie crust. Make a meringue by beating 3 egg whites until stiff. Gradually whisk in $\frac{1}{2}$ cup castor sugar and 1 tsp lemon juice. Pile on pudding and bake in a hot oven 8 to 10 minutes, or till brown. Serve cold.

APPLE PUDDING

Suet paste
Sliced dessert apples
2 tablespoonfuls sugar

Line a basin with suet pastry. Fill to the top with the apples and sprinkle with sugar. Cover with a suet pastry lid. Cover the basin with some greased paper. If you are boiling, tie with a pudding cloth also. Boil or steam for 2 $\frac{1}{2}$ or 3 hours.

EVE'S PUDDING

Roll out $\frac{1}{2}$ lb suet paste and sprinkle with chopped apple, brown sugar and currants. Roll up and bake in a hot oven for about 30 minutes.

JAM ROLY POLY

Roll out $\frac{1}{2}$ lb suet paste oblong shape spread with jam. Wet the edges and roll up. Tie in cloth and boil or place in baking tin and bake. Boil 1 $\frac{1}{2}$ hours.

Basic Recipe for Suet Pudding

This pudding can be served wi' golden syrup or jam, or even wi' meat an' stews, etc. This make 1/2 lb of dough.

8 ozs. flour

4 ozs. suet

A teaspoon salt

1 tablespoon baking powder

water

Chop the suet and rub into flour. Mix with enough water to mak' a stiff dough. The pudding can be boiled in a cloth or basin, steamed or baked.

If ye're boiling it, the basin must be filled and covered with a cloth and cooked for about 2 to 2 1/2 hours, depending on the recipe of course. If steamed, three-quarter fill the basin and cover with greased paper for the same time. If baked, put in a moderate oven for about 40 to 50 minutes.

If ye dinna like this
ye'll no' like onything!

Clootie Dumpling

Now <u>this</u> is something ye <u>must</u> be guid at. There's a lot o' ingredients here but this is the daddy o' dumplings. Be prepared for a lot o' work and a mess on the scullery flair.

4 oz suet, chopped

8 oz self-raising flour

1 teaspoon baking powder

4 oz breid crumbs

3 oz broon sugar

1 grated apple

8 oz currants and sultanas

1 teaspoon each of cinnamon, ginger, nutmeg

1 tablespoon golden syrup

2 eggs

Half fill a large pot and bring tae the boil. Scald a large piece of linen or cheesecloth with boiling water then dust it wi' flour. Beat the eggs, mix in the syrup and milk, and gradually mix into the dry ingredients and fruit. Place the mixture in the middle of the cloth. Tie it ticht but allow for swelling. Place an inverted plate on the bottom of the pan and put the pudding on it. Boil for 3 tae 4 hours. Never let the water drap ablow half the depth o' the pudding. Dip in cold water, remove the cloth and dry the pudding aff in a medium-tae-hot oven. Sprinkle the top wi' sugar and serve with cream or custard.

107

Gooseberry Trifle

1/2 pint gooseberry puree
3 or 4 small sponge cakes
1/2 pint custard
1/4 pint cream (thick)

Stew sufficient gooseberries to make a good pint, sweeten to taste, and sieve. Slice the sponge cakes and arrange in a glass dish. Pour the fruit over them and allow it to soak in. Make the custard with 1/2 pint milk, 1 egg, 1 oz. castor sugar, in the usual way. Then carefully stir 1/8 pint cream into it when it has cooled. Pour over the remainder of cream, whipped.

Baked Custard

2 eggs
2 small cups of milk
2 tsps sugar
Vanilla essence

Heat milk and pour on eggs which have been well beaten together with the sugar. Add a few drops of vanilla and pour into a well-buttered pie-dish and sprinkle a little grated nutmeg on top. Bake in a slow oven for about 3/4 of an hour. It is advisable to put pie-dish in a roasting tin with a little water.

Cream Custard

1 pt single cream
1 oz caster sugar
Yolks of 4 large eggs
1 teaspoon vanilla extract
2 teaspoon cornflour

Tae mak' the custard, heat the milk in a saucepan until it is beginning tae bubble, but dinna let it boil. Beat together the sugar, egg yolks and cornflour in a large bowl and tae this egg mixture gradually whisk in the hot milk with a balloon whisk. Add the vanilla extract. Once the eggs and milk are thoroughly whisked, pour the mixture back into the saucepan, over a gentle heat, and cook for around 8 minutes, still never allowing it tae boil. Either serve hot with your pudding or if making for a trifle, leave the custard tae cool while ye prepare the other ingredients. Bairns jist love trifle. I wonder whit yer ain bairnies will be like.

We love trifle

Mantha's Special Trifle

Before she got the boat to America my sister-in-law Mantha didnae hae such fancy ways! However, this is a braw trifle — though I dinna know if I approve o' a' the drink that's in it.

A dozen macaroons
1/2 cup cherry brandy (or sherry if you are normal and don't happen to have any cherry brandy in the hoose!)
1 guant cream custard
A dozen sponge fingers
1 pint of double cream
1/3 cup sugar
1/2 cup sherry (and the other half for herself nae doubt!)
A tin of black cherries, strained (or your own stewed cherries)

Put the macaroons in a glass trifle dish and pour ower the cherry brandy. Leave to soak. On top of this place the sponge fingers. Strain the cherries and place on top of the sponge. Retain a few for decoration. Prepare the custard, cool and pour ower. Allow to chill somewhere cool. Mix the cream wi' the sugar and the sherry, whip until stiff and decorate wi' a few cherries. Tastes best if chilled overnight in the "spring-house", according to Mantha. Those of us wi'oot a spring-hoose had mibbie best use a windae ledge!

Scotch Trifle (or Tipsy Laird)

This is no' really for bairnies with a' the liqueur that's in it. Make it without for them. AWW!

6 sponge cakes (or enough tae cover the bottom of the dish)

Raspberry jam

15 oz almond biscuits

6 tablespoons (or a right guid splash) of Drambuie (we aye keep a bottle, just for this ye ken)

2 soup bowls of raspberries

1 pint of cream custard (recipe on previous page)

10 fl oz double cream, whipped

Flaked almonds for topping

Spread the sponges wi' raspberry jam and place in the bottom of a glass trifle bowl. Break up the almond biscuits and sprinkle over the sponges. On top of this pour 6 tablespoons. of Drambuie. Ye can lick the spoon. On top of this spread the raspberries. If the custard is cooled then pour it over the raspberries and chill. Spread wi' whipped cream and cover wi' flaked almonds. Serves six, or fewer if yer greedy.

Mrs Frame's Coconut Pudding

1/2 pint milk

2 ozs. coconut

2 ozs. breadcrumbs

1 oz. castor sugar, plus 2 further tbsps

Grated lemon rind

1 oz. butter

2 eggs, separated

Make the breadcrumbs and add to a bowl. Boil the milk and pour over breadcrumbs. To this add butter, sugar, coconut, and a little lemon rind. Beat the egg yolks, and add when the mixture is cooled a little. Bake in a moderate oven until set. Then make meringue. Whip 2 egg whites till stiff, then add 2 tbsps sugar gradually to them. Pile the meringue roughly on top of pudding. Cook in a hot oven for about 8 to ten minutes or till browned.

Cherry and Apple Pudding

4 oz. flour

4 oz. breadcrumbs

4 oz. butter

4 oz. apples

2 oz. glace cherries

2 oz. mixed peel

milk to mix

3 oz. sugar

1 egg

Pare and chop up apples. Chop peel and cut up cherries. Mix all dry ingredients together, rub in butter. Mix with egg and milk. Pour into greased basin, cover with greased paper. Steam 1 1/2 to 2 hours.

Nº 23

MACDUFF'S
SCOTTISH FOODS OF QUALITY

Ingredients:
1 lb. stoned raisins	½ lb. sugar
1 lb. currants	½ lb. flour
½ lb. sultanas	1 lb. bread crumbs
3 ozs. chopped almonds	1 lb. suet
¼ lb. citron	4 eggs
¼ lb. candied peel	2 gills milk
¼ lb. grated carrot	1 teaspoonful salt

METHOD: Clean all fruit, blanch and chop almonds, grate the carrot, chop the citron and candied peel. Cream the suet and sugar, add eggs, then bread crumbs and flour and milk, then all the other ingredients, and mix very well. Steam for 6 hours or boil for 4 hours. This will keep for several weeks if necessary.

Plum Pudding

GROOO! We haTe
Semolina

Semolina

Did you know that dry semolina can be used in biscuits and pastry tae mak' them crunchier? Well it can. Semolina is a cheap, easy pudding to make. Though it's never been ane of my favourites it is useful to know how to make it and it is guid for filling hungry wee bellies.

1 1/2 oz. semolina

1 oz. sugar

1 egg

1 pint milk

semolina wi rasp jam on top is braw!

Heat the milk and sprinkle in the semolina, stirring a' the time. Cook till the grain is thick (7 tae 10 minutes should dae it). Add sugar and, when it's cooled, add beaten egg. Then the stiffly beaten egg white should be folded in. Pour into a buttered ashet and cook in a hot oven for 20 minutes.
   Ither wee grains can be cooked in the same way.

Elderberry Jelly Sweet

Elderberries
Stewed apples
Sugar (1/2 lb for every pint of juice)
Cornflour (scant 2 oz. for every pint of juice)

Remove all the stalks and put the berries into a large jar and place in large pan of boiling water to extract the juice. Crush with a wooden spoon, strain through a muslin cloth, and squeeze out the juice. To each pint of juice add 1/2 lb. sugar. Bring to the boil, and simmer very gently for five minutes. Thicken with cornflour (mix the cornflour with a little juice in a cup and then add to the rest of the mixture). Pour into individual glasses and leave to cool. When it has set, cover with stewed apples and top with whipped cream.

Mixed Fruit Cocktail

2 grapefruit
3 bananas
2 ozs. sugar
1 orange
1/2 lb. raspberries
1 oz. crystallised ginger

Cut grapefruit in half. Scoop pulp of orange and grapefruit into basin. Pick raspberries and add, keeping back eight of best. Chop ginger and add to fruit with sugar to taste. Slice bananas thinly. Fill grapefruit skins with mixed fruit, arrange a circle of banana on top and put two raspberries in centre.

Rice Pudding

A teaspoonful of fine oatmeal gies a creamy texture to rice pudding. I love the skin on the top, don't you? Ye'll find that efter a' yer work, my laddie will probably be mair interested in the crusty bits roon' the rim o' the dish. He always has liked that.

1 1/2 oz. rice
1 pint milk
1 dessertspoon granulated sugar
Grated nutmeg

Grease an oven dish. Wash the rice using a sieve and put in the dish. Mix the sugar with the milk and pour over the rice. Grate a little nutmeg over the top an' bake in a moderate oven for about 2 hours. If the milk dries up too much, add a little more.

This is also lovely with sultanas in it. Add at the start.

CURRANT LOAF

You can add an ounce of mixed peel to this recipe if desired and reduce the currants to 7 oz.

14 oz plain flour
2 tsps baking powder
1 tsp bicarbonate of soda
4 oz butter
8 oz caster sugar
5 oz raisins
8 oz currants
1/2 pint buttermilk

Use a 2-lb loaf tin. Preheat the oven to 350°F. Sieve the flour and baking powder into a bowl, then rub in the butter with your fingers. Add the sugar and also blend this through with your fingers. Add the dried fruit and mix thoroughly. Bind the mixture together with the sour milk. Grease the loaf tin and line with baking parchment. Fill the loaf tin with the mixture and bake at 350°F for one hour. Reduce the heat to 325°F for a further hour. Test the loaf with a skewer after about 40 minutes. It is best to store the loaf in an airtight container for two days before cutting and spreading with butter.

If indigestion you daily dread --- Eat less MEAT and more CURRANT BREAD

Have some for tea To-day!

Central Currant Office (London),
Advertisement Department,
10-13, New Bridge Street, E.C.4.

"GET IT AT ANDERSON'S."
HAIR DYE, in Auburn, Blonde, Brown, and Black Colours. SAFE and SPEEDY. Bottles, 1/3 each. Postage 6d. extra.
HAIR RESTORER, Renews Grey and Faded

Cranachan or Cream Crowdie

Double cream
Coarse toasted oatmeal
Castor sugar
Rum or vanilla
Fresh seasonal berries

Toast some oatmeal lightly in the oven, or in a thick-bottomed frying-pan over a gentle heat. This gives it a nutty taste.

Beat a bowlful of cream to a stiff froth, and stir in a handful or two of oatmeal, making it not too substantial, i.e., the cream must predominate. Sweeten to taste, and flavour with rum or vanilla seeds.

Throw in a few handfuls of fresh ripe berries— strawberries, blaeberries, raspberries, brambles, or others.

Breid and Butter Pudding

Stale biscuits or dry white cake can be used instead o breid, and a sprinkle o' sugar on top afore it's baked makes a braw crispy crust!

1 egg yolk

1 tablespoon sugar

1/2 pint milk

2 slices thin breid and butter

1 oz. currants

Dissolve the sugar in the milk and simmer till bubbling but not boiling, stirring till the sugar is disolved. Beat the egg yolk in a bowl and add the warm milk to the bowl. Return the mixture to the pan and simmer, stirring continuously. Do not boil! Strain and set aside. Cut the breid and butter into small pieces, and lay it in a buttered oven dish. Sprinkle currants in between. Some folk add mixed peel, but I hate mixed peel. Pour the custard over the breid and let it soak in for half an hour. Bake in a moderate-to-hot oven for about 30 tae 40 minutes or until the pudding is risen and set.

With all recipes sieve the Flour

SHORTBREAD

8 ozs. IMPERIAL Plain Flour	4 ozs. Butter
	2 ozs. Castor Sugar

Keeping all ingredients cool, work the sugar into the butter, on a board and with the fingers until well mixed, add the flour and knead together. Press into a round sandwich tin, prick right through all over and score the edge to decorate. Bake in a *very* slow oven until biscuit coloured.

IMPERIAL BISCUITS

8 ozs. IMPERIAL Plain Flour	1 Teaspoonful Cinnamon
4 ozs. Sugar	¼ Teaspoonful Baking Powder
4 ozs. Butter	¼ Teaspoonful Salt
1 Egg	Jam

Cream the butter and sugar, add beaten egg, sieved flour, baking powder, salt and cinnamon, knead until smooth. Turn on to a floured board and roll thinly. Cut into rounds and bake on greased tins in a moderate oven. Spread icing on half the number of biscuits and jam on the other half. Place together and decorate with small pieces of cherry.

CHERRY CAKES

6 ozs. IMPERIAL Plain Flour	2 ozs. Cherries
4 ozs. Sugar	Milk if necessary
4 ozs. Margarine	1 Teaspoonful Baking Powder
2 Eggs	

Cut the cherries into small pieces. Cream the fat and sugar, add the beaten eggs and sieve in the flour and baking powder. Slowly add cherries and spoon into greased patty tins and bake in moderate oven for 10-17 mins.

POTATO SCONES

2 ozs. IMPERIAL Plain Flour	¼ Teaspoonful Salt
8 ozs. Cold mashed Potato	Milk
1 oz. Butter	

Mash potatoes with butter and a little milk, beat for a few minutes with a wooden spoon, add flour and salt. Roll out very thinly, cut and place on hot girdle for about 5 mins. turning when half cooked.

HAVE YOU TRIED DOUGLAS' ROLLED OATS?

FLAPJACKS

8 ozs. Douglas' Rolled Oats	2 Tablespoons Golden Syrup
4 ozs. Margarine	Salt
2 ozs. Brown Sugar	

Place oats, salt and sugar in a basin. Melt margarine and syrup in pan then stir into the dry ingredients. Turn into a shallow greased tin, bake in moderate oven for 20-25 mins. Cut into fingers, leaving in tray until cold.

Pastry

Maggie, making pastry is an art and it
taks a light hand tae mak' it guid — ye
canna be slapdash wi' ony kind of baking.
Be awfy accurate in how ye measure — nae
guessing — it's no' like making soup. Keep
your ingredients as cold as possible. Handle it
as little as possible and cook in a high oven.

SUET PUDDINGS

BASIC RECIPE FOR SUET PUDDINGS

8 ozs. flour
4 ozs. suet
pinch of salt
water

Chop suet and rub into flour. Mix to a stiff dough with water. If less than 4 ozs. of suet to 1/2 lb. flour is used add 1/2 teaspoonful baking powder. Half flour and half self-raising flour can also be used and no baking powder.

Made with self-raising flour the paste can be divided into small portions and dropped into boiling water for 20 minutes.

These dumplings can be served with meat stews, etc., or served plain with golden syrup or jam.

The pudding can be boiled in a cloth or basin, steamed or baked.

If boiled, the basin must be filled and covered with a cloth. If steamed—three-quarter fill the basin and cover with greased paper. If baked put in a moderate oven.

A Good Meal

A STEAK and Kidney Pudding, without a trace of toughness in the crust, enjoyed to the last bite for the rich meat flavour of its gravy; and an apple pie with the delicious short crust that only

Hugon's
'ATORA'
The Good BEEF SUET

can make; what a feast for the epicure!

If you do not know what "Atora" cookery is like, a meal like that will be a revelation to you. And "Atora" as it is perfectly shredded, saves an enormous amount of trouble compared with raw suet.

Sold at all first-class Grocers, in 2d. and 4-oz. 8-oz. and 1/-oz. Write for our free booklet to tested recipes; they are

HUGON & CO., LTD., M

The proprietors of Refined Beef Suet

"Atora" contains no pr

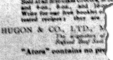

A ~~Boon~~ BROON in the Kitchen

BISTO doubles the housewife's opportunities for securing a variety of appetising and nourishing dishes.

A little Bisto stirred into Soups and Stews when boiling makes a wonderful improvement — and Meat Puddings and Pies are all the nicer when Bisto is used.

A 3d. Packet lasts a family a week.

Also in larger cartons and in tins.

BISTO
for all Meat Dishes

Ha Ha
Very funny
Horace

120

Suet Crust Pastry

This is a good short pastry for savoury pies.

1 lb. flour

6-8 oz. suet

1 teaspoon salt

2 teaspoon baking powder

Cold water

Sieve the flour. Shred and chop the suet finely. Add the salt and baking powder tae the flour and mix with suet. Add the cold water tae this mixture and mix till it becomes an elastic dough. Dust a board wi' flour and roll as required.

Hot Water Crust Pastry

1 lb. flour

5-6 oz. lard

3/8 pint (1 1/2 gills) water

1 teasp. salt

Boil water and lard, stir into flour and salt. Knead until smooth. Use for Scotch pies and the like.

Genoese Pastry Cakes

4 eggs
3 ozs. butter (or the same weight as the eggs)
3 ozs. flour (or the same weight as the eggs)
3 ozs. sugar (or the same weight as the eggs)
3 ozs. ground almonds
Butter icing
Water icing

Sift the flour. Beat the eggs and sugar together in a basin over some hot water until light and frothy. Melt the butter. Let the butter become the same temperature as the egg-and-sugar mixture. This is an important step. Stir the butter in lightly. Fold in the sifted flour and, lastly, the ground almonds. Turn into a greased shallow baking tin. Bake in a moderate oven for about 30 to 40 minutes. While still hot, cut into small shapes. When cool spread with ~~the~~ chocolate, coffee, or vanilla butter icing. I like fresh whipped cream too. Place another slice on top. Spread with more filling. Add another slice. Press lightly. Pour over water icing.

Short Crust Pastry

Add a wee dash of sugar for sweet pies.

1 lb. flour
8 oz. butter, or butter and lard
1/2 teaspoon salt
Cold water

Sieve the flour. Cut fat into cubes, add tae the flour and using awfy cold hands (chill them in cauld water if ye can) rub the fat into the flour tae mak' the mixture look like breid crumbs. Add salt and sufficient cold water tae mak' a stiff dough. Roll out once. Tae keep this light, dinna over handle your dough or allow tae get warm

Oatmeal Pastry

This is awfy easy and is made in the same way as the short crust, but you need to use equal quantities of flour and oatmeal.

Choux Pastry

2 ¹/₂ ozs. sifted flour

2 eggs

1 oz. butter

¹/₄ pint water

¹/₄ tsp. vanilla extract

Pinch salt

1 tsp. castor sugar

Boil the water and butter in a pan; sift the flour and add to boiling liquid. Keep on the heat and beat the mixture until smooth and leaving the sides of the pan, stirring all the time. Allow to cool slightly, then add the beaten eggs gradually. Keep beating, then add vanilla extract. Choux pastry should be cooked in a high oven for about 30 minutes depending on the size of the cakes you are making. This patry needs to be piped and makes about 12 choux buns.

CHOCOLATE ECLAIRS

Choux pastry
Whipped cream
Chocolate icing

Pipe finger-lengths of pastry onto a buttered baking tray. Cook in a high oven for about 30 minutes or until light brown. When cooked, split and remove the soft inside; fill with whipped cream or pastry custard. Ice with chocolate icing.

Rough Puff Pastry

This is slightly easier to make than and a wee bit rougher than Flaky Pastry. Probably best for savoury dishes, leaving Flaky for sweet dishes.

1 lb. flour
10—12 oz. butter or butter and lard
1/2 teaspoon salt
Cold water

Measure flour and add salt. Cut fat intae wee bits. Mix tae elastic consistency wi' the cold water. Roll into strip on floured board. Fold up 1/3 and down 1/3 and seal edges. Half turn so that open ends are top and bottom and roll out again. Repeat three times, then use as desired.

Flaky Pastry

The lemon juice is vital for this pastry so make sure you include it.

1/2 lb. flour

Pinch salt

3 oz. butter

3 oz. lard

1/2 teaspoon lemon juice

Cold water

Mix the lard and butter. Rub a quarter of the fat into the flour. Add the lemon juice and water and mix tae an elastic dough. Working lightly, roll the dough into a strip on a floured surface. Then a' ye dae is put a quarter of fat in small pats on twa-thirds of strip. Flour lightly, fold on itself in three, turn and roll into a strip again. Repeat a couple o' times mair wi' the remaining fat. Set aside if possible for half an hour tae cool. Roll and fold twice then use as required.

CHOCOLATE CAKE

1/4 lb. butter
1/4 lb. flour
1/4 lb. castor sugar
1/4 lb. chocolate
1/2 teaspoonful baking powder
1 teaspoonful vanilla essence
1 tablespoonful ground rice,
2 eggs

Method. — Beat the butter till soft, mix in the sugar and beat to a cream, add the chocolate broken up and melted over the fire in 3 tablespoonfuls of water, mix in the yolks separately, beat well, then add the flour, baking powder and ground rice, drop in a teaspoonful vanilla, and lastly, stir in the whites of eggs beaten till quite stiff. Bake for about 3/4 to 1 hour in a moderate oven.

Icing. — Melt 3 oz. chocolate in 1/2 gill of water over the fire, boil for 5 minutes, then cool a little, and add 1/2 lb. icing sugar rubbed through a hair sieve. Stir over very gentle heat for a few seconds to take chill off, then pour over cake.

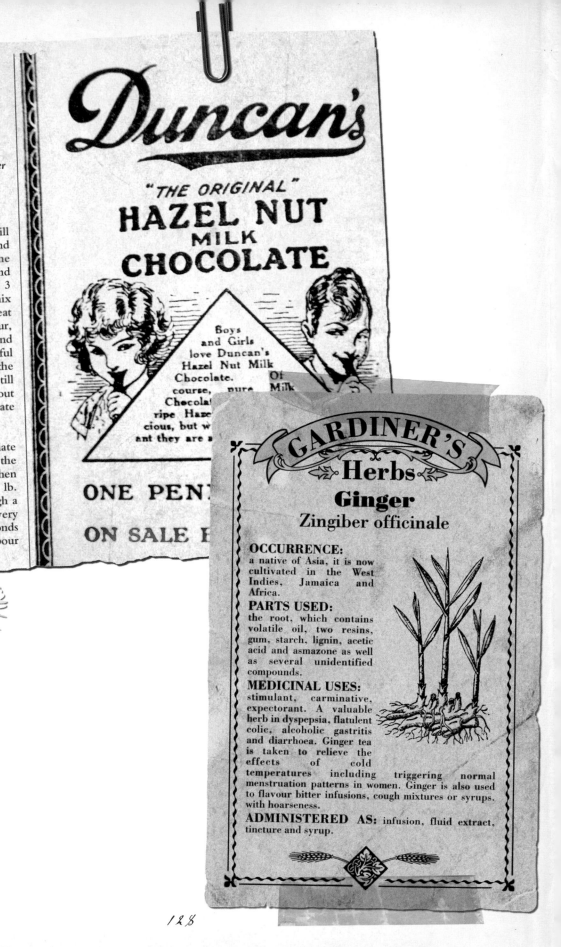

Duncan's

"THE ORIGINAL" HAZEL NUT MILK CHOCOLATE

Boys and Girls love Duncan's Hazel Nut Milk Chocolate. Of course, pure Milk Chocolate ripe Haze... cious, but w... ant they are ...

ONE PENN...

ON SALE ...

GARDINER'S Herbs

Ginger
Zingiber officinale

OCCURRENCE:
a native of Asia, it is now cultivated in the West Indies, Jamaica and Africa.

PARTS USED:
the root, which contains volatile oil, two resins, gum, starch, lignin, acetic acid and asmazone as well as several unidentified compounds.

MEDICINAL USES:
stimulant, carminative, expectorant. A valuable herb in dyspepsia, flatulent colic, alcoholic gastritis and diarrhoea. Ginger tea is taken to relieve the effects of cold temperatures including triggering normal menstruation patterns in women. Ginger is also used to flavour bitter infusions, cough mixtures or syrups. with hoarseness.

ADMINISTERED AS: infusion, fluid extract, tincture and syrup.

Baking

Baking can be rare fun, especially if you get your bairns to help. It's awfy tempting tae jist nip oot tae the baker's, but, I'm tellin' ye, ye jist canna beat the smell and the taste o' home-made scones and the like.

Raspberry Buns

We made these at school today.

6 oz. flour
pinch of salt
2 level tsps baking powder
3 oz. butter
2 oz. sugar
milk to mix
raspberry jam

Sift the flour, salt and baking powder. Rub the butter into the flour until it looks a bit like breadcrumbs. Add the sugar, and use enough milk to mix to a soft dough that is firm enough to roll out on a floured surface. Roll out to ¼ inch thick. Cut into rounds, using a cutter. Place a teaspoon of raspberry jam in the centre of each one, moisten the edges and gather the dough to cover the jam. Place them on a greased baking tray with the gathered side downwards. Mark a small cross on the centre of each, but don't cut right through the pastry. Bake in a hot oven for 20 minutes.

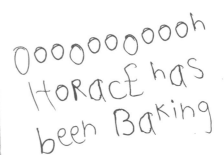

Oooooooooooh HORACE has been Baking

Raising agents

Proportions for plain baking

1. 1 tsp bicarbonate of soda
   1 teaspoonful cream of tartar
   1 lb. flour plus buttermilk

2. 1 tsp bicarbonate of soda
   2 teaspoonfuls cream of tartar
   1 lb. flour plus sweet milk

3. 2 teaspoonfuls baking powder
   1 lb. Flour plus sweet milk

Baking powder
2 oz. baking soda
4 oz. cream of tartar
6 oz. rice flour

Dropped Scones

Now dinna be drappin' them on the kitchen flair frae the hot tray. Ha ha! Jist my wee joke.

1 lb. flour

1 teaspoon bicarbonate of soda

1 teaspoon cream of tartar

1/2 teaspoon salt

2 oz casrter sugar or syrup

2 eggs

Milk or buttermilk to mix

Combine a' the dry ingredients. Beat the eggs and add to a well in the centre of dry mixture. Mix with as much milk tae make a soft, smooth batter. Grease a hot girdle with fat (dinna use butter — it micht burn). Drap a spoonful of the mixture on tae the girdle. My mither aye used an iron spoon and so dae I. When broon on ane side, turn and broon on the other. Leave tae cool on a wire tray and wrap in a clean tea towel. Serve with butter and home made jam. Oh, these are braw hot wi' butter an golden syrup!

PUFF SCONES

8 oz. flour
1 teaspoonful sugar
1 teaspoonful baking soda
2 ½ oz. lard
1 small tea cup milk (sour)
pinch of salt
1 teaspoonful cream of tartar

Mix flour, cream of tartar, baking soda, sugar and salt in a mixing bowl and rub in the margarine with the finger tips. Using a knife, stir in milk to make a soft dough. Knead very lightly, roll out ½ inch to ¾ inch thick and cut into rounds. Place on a floured baking tin and bake in hot oven for 10 minutes.

TO TAKE BRUISES OUT OF FURNITURE

Wet the part with warm water. Double a piece of brown paper six times thick. Soak it and lay it on the place. Apply on that a hot flat iron until the moisture is evaporated. If the bruise has not gone, repeat the process till the dent or bruise is raised level with the surface.

TO LOOSEN ARTICLES THAT HAVE BECOME FIXED

If tumblers become fixed, tap gently around with another tumbler, and like magic they will come apart. If a glass stopper is fixed, tap round it with another, and it will be loosened. If two flower-pots are fixed, tap with another flower-pot. If two iron screws, tap with piece of iron, and so on. You will always have the same result. The rule is tap each article with one of similar kind.

Ankle Cl...
by skilful...
men, "Ba...
stoutly resists...

Ballit...

O'Brien Gramophones
ON FREE APPROVAL

My free lists only want seeing, and you will not buy elsewhere. Small deposit gets any horn or hornless model by return on 14 Days' Approval, Packed Free and Carriage Paid. Money refunded if dissatisfied. Write at once for free lists. I am one of the oldest advertisers in this paper.

O'Brien
THE WORLD'S LARGEST CYCLE DEALER DEP 46 COVENTRY.

Treacle Scones

1 lb. flour
2 ozs. butter
2 tbsps treacle
1 tsp bicarbonate of soda
1 tsp ground cinnamon
1 ½ tbsp sugar
1 tsp mixed spice
Salt
Buttermilk to mix (half teaspoon cream of tartar may be added if sweet milk is used)

Mix the fat and dry ingredients as you do in the sweet scone recipe. Add the treacle, then begin to mix with buttermilk until a stiff dough. Divide this one into four and place on a greased tray. Glaze with milk or egg is if you wish. Bake in a hot oven for 12 to 15 minutes.

Sweet Milk Scones

1/2 lb. flour

1/2 oz. sugar

1 oz. butter

1 teaspoon cream of tartar

1/2 teaspoon bicarbonate of soda

1/2 teaspoon salt

1/4 pint milk

Rub the butter into the flour. Keep your hands cool and keep the mixing of this as light as possible. What I mean by that is see if ye can get as much air into the mixture as ye can. Add the rest o' the dry ingredients, and mix into a light dough with the milk. Turn the dough out on tae a floured board. Handle it as little as possible. Roll it out lightly and cut in eight pieces. Lay on a greased baking tray. Glaze the scones wi' a brush o' egg or milk (I like them a bit floury masel'). Bake in a hot oven for 10 minutes.

Plain White Cake

6 to 8 ozs. butter

6 to 8 ozs. sugar

1 lb. flour

2 large eggs, separated

2 teaspoons baking powder

Milk

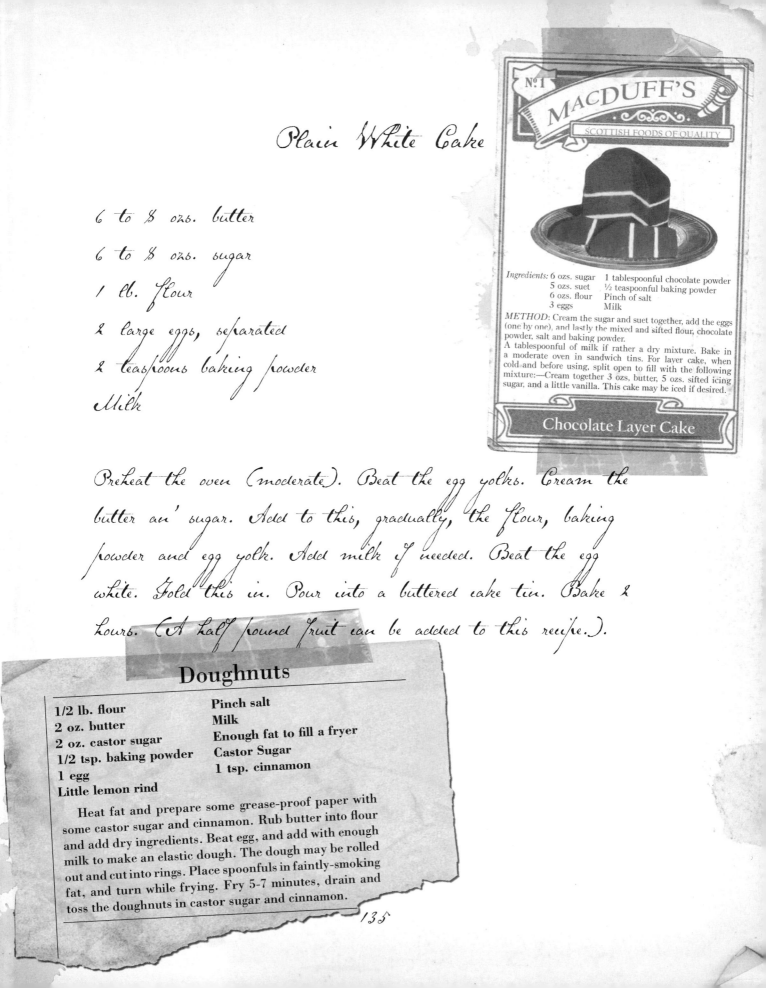

MacDUFF'S
Nº 1
SCOTTISH FOODS OF QUALITY

Ingredients: 6 ozs. sugar   1 tablespoonful chocolate powder
5 ozs. suet   ½ teaspoonful baking powder
6 ozs. flour   Pinch of salt
3 eggs   Milk

METHOD: Cream the sugar and suet together, add the eggs (one by one), and lastly the mixed and sifted flour, chocolate powder, salt and baking powder.
A tablespoonful of milk if rather a dry mixture. Bake in a moderate oven in sandwich tins. For layer cake, when cold and before using, split open to fill with the following mixture:—Cream together 3 ozs. butter, 5 ozs. sifted icing sugar, and a little vanilla. This cake may be iced if desired.

Chocolate Layer Cake

Preheat the oven (moderate). Beat the egg yolks. Cream the butter an' sugar. Add to this, gradually, the flour, baking powder and egg yolk. Add milk if needed. Beat the egg white. Fold this in. Pour into a buttered cake tin. Bake 2 hours. (A half pound fruit can be added to this recipe.)

Doughnuts

1/2 lb. flour
2 oz. butter
2 oz. castor sugar
1/2 tsp. baking powder
1 egg
Little lemon rind

Pinch salt
Milk
Enough fat to fill a fryer
Castor Sugar
1 tsp. cinnamon

    Heat fat and prepare some grease-proof paper with some castor sugar and cinnamon. Rub butter into flour and add dry ingredients. Beat egg, and add with enough milk to make an elastic dough. The dough may be rolled out and cut into rings. Place spoonfuls in faintly-smoking fat, and turn while frying. Fry 5-7 minutes, drain and toss the doughnuts in castor sugar and cinnamon.

Slab Cake

10 ozs Flour, 6 ozs butter, ½ lb. Gran; sugar.
6 = Currants 6 = Sultanas or Sunmaid
raisins, 4 ozs mixed peel 4 eggs 1 teaspoonful
Bak: Powder 2 ozs Almonds. ½ teaspoon; Mixed Spice
Beat Butter & sugar to a cream, then add
eggs, a pinch of salt, spice, chop the peel finely
then fruit & flour, & bake in a moderate
hot oven 2½ to 3 hours. begin to lessen
the heat after the first hour.

Cut the sultanas or raisins in half.
either ground almonds or whole almonds
chopped fine may be used.

The cake is much improved if made
night before, baking; adding bak. Powder
before placing in oven.

MACDUFF'S
SCOTTISH FOODS OF QUALITY
№ 7

Ingredients: ½ lb. flour ½ lb. oatmeal 6 ozs. suet 4 ozs. brown sugar Pinch of salt 1 teacup of syrup 2 eggs 1 teaspoonful of ginger 1 teaspoonful carbonate of soda in a little warm milk

METHOD: Rub the suet into the flour and mix all dry ingredients, add eggs, syrup, milk, and carbonate of soda. Beat thoroughly, and bake in a flat tin.

Gingerbread

COBURG CAKES

1 cup flour
¼ lb. butter
½ cup sugar
2 eggs
1 tbsp milk
1 tbsp treacle
Hot water to mix
½ tsp ground ginger
¼ tsp ground cloves
1 level tsp mixed spice
1 level tsp cinnamon
1 heaped tsp baking powder
Some whole almonds

Cream the butter and sugar and mix with the flour, baking powder, and spices. Add the the eggs, and milk, and then mix the treacle in a little hot water to make it easier to mix. Bake on the middle shelf of a quick oven in well-buttered patty tins. Put a whole almond in the bottom of each tin. Bake for about 15 minutes.

Ginger Sandwiches

Margaret Purdie tell me aboot these. These are no' as fancy as they look but they are braw. A bit like me! They are easy tae mak' and will impress yer visitors. Well, they impress Mrs Gow but then she gets excited aboot tinned corned beef. No" that I've got onything against corned beef, ye understand.

Preserved ginger
Guid, quite soft, broon breid and unsalted butter
Cream

Cut the crusts off the bread and spread with unsalted butter. Thinly slice or grate the preserved ginger. Whip the cream till it's richt stiff. Mix the ginger loosely wi" the cream and spread on the broon breid and butter. Cut into fancy shapes or roll the breid (like a Swiss roll) and cut into circles which ye pin with wooden skewers if ye've got any. Wee triangles are just as genteel so dinna worry if you don't.

137

Daphne's Chocolate Cake

1/4 lb. butter
1/4 lb. flour
1/4 lb. castor sugar
1/4 lb. chocolate
1/2 tsp. baking powder
1 tsp. vanilla extract
1 tbsp. ground rice,
2 egg yolks
2 egg whites beaten till stiff
1/4 pint double cream, whipped

Beat the butter till soft, mix in the sugar and beat to a cream, add the chocolate broken up and melted over the fire in 3 tablespoonfuls of water, mix in the yolks separately, beat well, then add the flour, baking powder and ground rice, drop in a teaspoonful vanilla, and lastly, stir in beaten egg whites of eggs. Bake for about 3/4 to 1 hour in a moderate oven. Allow to cool and slice the cake into two circles. Fill with whipped cream.

Icing.—Melt 3 oz. chocolate in 1/2 gill of water over the fire, boil for 5 minutes, then cool a little, and add 1/2 lb. icing sugar rubbed through a hair sieve. Stir over very gentle heat for a few seconds to take chill off, then pour over cake.

Calories: 100 cals per slice

Chocolate Cake

½ lb butter.
½ lb plain chocolate.
2 ozs ground rice
1 teaspoonful vanilla essence.
2 dessertspoonful milk.
1 teaspoonful baking powder.

6 ozs castor sugar
4 ozs flour
4 eggs.

Melt butter & sugar: beat eggs & add. Then add melted chocolate and milk warmed add flour, rice & essence, and lastly baking powder. Put into tin lined with greased paper and bake in slow oven for 1 hour

Em ... that must be one TINY bit of cake Daphne! More like 500 calories a slice

Dundee Cake

Wi' aw' these ingredients, this micht seem ower complicated but it's worth a' the effort. It's delicious.

8 oz. butter

2 oz. cut peel

2 oz. glace cherries

1 cup currants

3 eggs

1 1/2 cups flour

1 cup broon sugar

A pinch of salt

1 cup sultanas

1 tablespoon milk

1/4 teaspoon mixed spice

2 oz. blanched almonds (for top)

2 teaspoon baking powder

Mix together and sift the flour, baking powder, salt, and spices. Cream the butter and sugar, and beat in ane egg at a time, adding with each ane, a tablespoonful of the flour mixture. When the eggs are thoroughly beaten in add the remainder o' the flour mixture with the milk. Then add the fruit and mix the whole well. Pour into a lined tin, cover the top wi' almonds, and bake on the middle shelf of a moderate oven for 2 hours.

Sponge Cake (Economical)

2 tbsps dried egg
2 oz. sugar
1 tsp baking powder
4 tbsps water
4 tbsps flour
A little milk
Vanilla extract

Mix the egg and water, add sugar and essence and beat well. Then fold in the flour. Pour into a tin and bake in a warm oven for 15-20 minutes.

Easy Sponge Cake

5 oz. sugar
1/4 lb. butter
4 eggs
1/2 lb. self-raising flour

cream 5 oz. sugar with 1/4 lb. butter, beating very well. Beat in 4 eggs, one at a time for fully 3 minutes. When the last one is in, beat for 5 minutes, then sift in 1/2 lb. self-raising flour. Mix well, then put into a tin lined with greaseproof paper. Bake in a moderate oven for 1 hour.

Good Sponge Cake

5 eggs
the weight of 4 eggs in sugar
the weight of 3 eggs in flour,
and flavouring

Beat eggs and sugar to a cream, add flour very gently, and a few drops of any essence. Bake in moderate oven for about 1 hour.

Butter Sponge Cake

This is a nice rich sponge. I like it spread with whipped cream and sometimes, as an alternative, butter icing (whip 5 cups of icing sugar with 1 cup of butter. If the mixture is too stiff add a tablespoon milk).

1/2 lb. flour

1/2 lb. sugar

1/4 lb. butter

2 eggs

1/2 teacupful milk

1 teaspoonful cream of tartar

1/2 teaspoonful bi-carbonate of soda

Beat butter and sugar, add eggs one at a time, then add the flour and powders, and right at the end, the milk. Line and butter two sandwich tins and divide the mixture. Bake for 1/2 an hour on the middle shelf a quick oven.

Fill with whipped cream and jam and sift icing sugar on top.

Swiss Tarts

Nº 18

MACDUFF'S

SCOTTISH FOODS OF QUALITY

Pastry Ingredients:
1 lb. flour
5 ozs. suet
¼ lb. butter
Pinch of salt
Mix with water

Filling Ingredients:
¼ lb. ground rice
¼ lb. castor sugar
2 ozs. suet
1 egg
A few drops of vanilla

METHOD: 1 teaspoonful of raspberry jam at the bottom of the tart before the filling is put in.
For raspberry tarts, fill with raspberry jam; or lemon cheese may be used.

Jumbles

Nº 8

MACDUFF'S

SCOTTISH FOODS OF QUALITY

Ingredients: 8 ozs. flour   Grated rind of 1 lemon
6 ozs. sugar   1 egg
4 ozs. suet   Salt

METHOD: Beat the suet well. Mix the egg and sugar together, then mix all with a fork. Add the salt, flour and rind. Cut and roll into form with the hand, using sugar instead of flour. Bake in a moderate oven.

Edinburgh Tart

2 oz. butter
2 oz. sugar
2 oz. chopped candied peel
1 tbsp sultana
2 beaten eggs
Puff pastry

Line a buttered plate with some good puff pastry, pour in the following mixture and bake in a quick oven for a few minutes:—
Melt 2 oz. butter and 2 oz. sugar in a pan, add 2 oz. chopped candied peel, 1 dessertspoonful of sultana raisins and 2 beaten eggs. Small tartlets may be made using patty tins.

REGAL RECORDS

2 6

The Finest Grand Opera Record Ever Offered at Half-a-Crown

G 8704 { FAUST—Soldiers' Chorus .... } GRAND OPERA
{ FAUST—'Gainst the Power .... } CHORUS

For Xmas Get the Wonderful "Regal" List. Surface Smooth as Glass.

Keep warmer

Swiss Roll

If the sponge cracks a wee bit as you roll it up, dinna worry, you can sift a bit extra icing sugar over it to hide it.

4 oz. flour

4 oz. sugar

3 eggs

1 tablespoonful cold water

1 teaspoonful cream of tartar

1/2 teaspoonful baking soda

3 teaspoonfuls melted butter

Break the eggs into a bowl and beat lightly, then add cold water and sugar. Whisk over a pan of hot water till thick and creamy for about 15 minutes. Watch it doesn't curdle! Mix soda and cream of tartar with flour and sift gradually into mixture. Then stir in the melted butter carefully. Place in a greased oblong tin and bake in a moderate oven till firm. Turn out ontae paper sprinkled with icing sugar. Spread with warmed jam. (You could also spread with thickly whipped cream.) Roll up using the paper to help you do this and leave till cold. Slice and serve with pouring cream and fruit.

Black Bun

1 lb. flour
2 lbs. currants
2 lbs. raisins
1/2 lb. almonds
1/2 lb. mixed candied peel
4 oz. sugar
1/2 oz. ground ~~~~ cinnamon
1/2 oz. ground ginger

Small tsp bicarbonate of soda
1-2 tbsps brandy
Buttermilk to bind

Crust:
1 lb. Flour
1/2 lb. Butter
Water

Sift the flour into a basin, and add the sugar, spices, and prepared fruits. Add the brandy. Stir the soda into the buttermilk. Use this to moisten the cake – don't make it too wet.

Make the crust. Rub the butter into the flour and add enough water to make a stiff pastry dough. Roll out thinly. Grease a large cake-tin and line it evenly with the pastry dough. Keep enough to cover the top.

Trim the edges, spoon the cake mixture in. Put the lid of pastry dough on top. Make about four holes right down to the bottom of the cake with a long skewer. Prick the top all over with a fork, brush with beaten egg, and bake in a moderate oven for about four hours.

This cake should be made several weeks, or even months, before it is to be cut, which is usually at Hogmanay!

Biscuits

Once you get the hang o' this, ye'll be bakin' biscuits a' yer life, lassie.

3 oz. castor sugar

4 oz. butter

1 beaten egg

6 oz. flour

Cream the butter and sugar. Add the flour and mix it in well. Add enough egg tae mak' a stiff paste. Knead well and roll to about 1/4 in. thick. Cut into shapes, prick and bake on greased tin in moderate oven until pale broon. Cool on wire tray. Here's some ither biscuits that can be made jist by addin' these ingredients:—

Lemon—1 tablespoon grated lemon rind.

Ginger—1 teaspoon ground ginger.

Carraway—1 teaspoon carraway seeds.

Chocolate—1 tablespoon chocolate powder.

Maggie

The Gingerette recipe is no' very clear. This is what I do:

Cream the syrup, marg. and sugar in a bowl over a pan of hot water. Let it cool. Beat the egg and mix in alternate spoons of egg and flour to the sugar cream. Roll into balls and press flat on a baking tray. Bake 20 mins at 325 F.

Gingerette Biscuits

12 oz S.R. Flour.
6 or 7 oz. sugar.
3 oz syrup
4 " marg.
2 rounded teasp. Ginger
1 " " B. Soda
1 egg.

Heat syrup, marg. & sugar all in bowl in cream. Let cool. Mix dry ingred. & beat in turn. Roll into small balls & place on tray well apart. Bake 30 mins at 3.

Abernethy Biscuits

250 g/8 oz flour
1 level tsp cream of tartar
1 level tsp baking soda
75 g/3 oz butter
25 g/1 oz lard
75 g/3 oz sugar
1 tbsp milk
1 egg, beaten
Pinch of salt

Sieve the flour and the raising agents. Cut the fat into cubes and sprinkle into the flour. With cold hands (run them under the cold tap if they are too warm) and with a light touch rub the fat into the flour until it reaches a breadcrumb consistency. Add the sugar and mix until evenly distributed. Add the milk and enough beaten egg to form into a stiff dough. Roll till about 6 mm/ ¼ inch thick and cut into biscuits. Prick the surface of the biscuits with a fork and bake at 190ºC/375ºF/gas mark 5 for around 15 minutes or until golden brown.

Nº 6

MACDUFF'S
SCOTTISH FOODS OF QUALITY

Ingredients: 1 lb. flour   1 teaspoonful ginger
½ lb. sugar   1 teaspoonful carbonate of soda
6 ozs. suet   1 egg
½ lb. syrup   Salt

METHOD: Melt the suet and syrup. Mix all the dry ingredients, add the egg, then the melted suet and syrup. Put on a greased baking tin the size of a walnut and flatten with the hand.

Ginger Nuts

Butteries

1 lb plain flour	8 oz soft white fat or butter
2 oz fresh yeast	4 oz lard or solid vegetable fat
2 oz caster sugar	1/2 pint tepid water

Sieve the flour onto your work surface. Dissolve the sugar in the water and then crumble the yeast into the water and mix thoroughly. Takin' yer time, mix the liquid with the flour using a fork. Once a' the liquid is combined with the flour, knead the mixture until it's smooth and elastic. Score the dough with a cross and place in a bowl in a warm place tae rise for around 1 hour (this is called 'proving'). Knead the dough again, briefly and awfy lightly. Cream together the twa fats wi' a wooden spoon. Roll out the dough. Spread the top twa thirds of the dough with ane third of the fat. Fold the bottom third up over the middle and then fold the top third over. Leave for 30 minutes and repeat the process twice mair wi' the rest of the fat, but turn the dough. Leave the dough tae rest in a cool place after each rolling. Divide into 15 ovals and place on greased, floured baking trays, leaving space for them tae rise. Bake in a hot oven for 20 tae 25 minutes till risen.

147.

Sauces, Chutneys, Pickles, Preserves, Jam

Hints on Jam Making

The preserving-pan should be thick enough to prevent burning, and must be scrupulously clean.

If an enamelled pan is used, great care must be taken. Jams burn very readily in this. It is advisable to use it on the hot plate of a kitchener or else place an asbestos mat between it and the gas.

Stir carefully to avoid mashing the fruit. Jam that is sufficiently cooked will set in a very little space on a cold plate. Tilt the plate and the jam will take on a wrinkled appearance.

Overcooked jam will be sticky and lose flavour and colour.

Soft fruits, such as strawberries and raspberries, set better if a little acid fruit-juice is added, such as redcurrant. The amount required is 1 pint to very 4 lbs. of fruit.

Use a wooden spoon for jam, never an iron one.

JAM
Broon
1st
SCOTTISH WOMEN'S GUILD

The Equipment Required.
A preserving-pan, a long wooden spoon, scales for weighing, a pint or quart measure, a knife with a sharp point, a silver knife, and a flannel bag for straining jelly are about all that is required. No iron or tin should be allowed to come into contact with the raw fruit.

The Preserving-pan.
This should be made of copper, brass or aluminium. All the utensils used must be perfectly clean, and it is best to keep a pan and spoon specially for this purpose.

Jars for Potting.
When choosing the jars, the needs of the family should be considered, and the jars selected accordingly. Those with screw tops will simplify the process of covering.

Use only sound fresh fruit and pure granulated sugar. An inferior quality of sugar not only spoils the colour and flavour of the jam, but it throws up a lot of scum, which is wasteful. Use no preservatives, no colouring matter, and no glucose.

The Maturity of the Fruit.
This is an important point. As a rule every fruit is at its best for jam-making just before it is quite ripe. When fully matured it is not so satisfactory. The reason for this is that "pectin" the gelatinous principle which causes "setting", is at its best in fruit slightly under-ripe, and scarcely exists in that which is over-ripe.

Picking and Cleaning.
All fruit requires a certain amount of picking and cleaning before it can be used. It may be either wiped with a soft cloth or washed in water, according to the nature of the fruit. Very soft fruits, such as strawberries, raspberries, and loganberries, will not bear any handling beyond picking over. Gooseberries, cherries, and currants can all be washed, a few at a time, and drained in a colander. Plums can be either wiped or washed, according to whether they are soiled or not. Peaches and nectarines should have boiled water poured over them in order to remove the skins. All bruises and blemishes must, of course, be removed, and any over-ripe or squashy fruit discarded.

Jam from Soft Fruit.
When making jam from soft fruit, put the fruit and sugar into a preserving-pan and bring them quickly to the boil. Cook for 10 minutes, then add 1/2 oz. Butter. Do not skim the jam, as this is not necessary if pure sugar has been used. The butter will clear it and safe the waste of skimming. Allow, as a rule, 25 minutes cooking from the time the jam comes to the boil, but it should be tested before that by trying to little on a plate.

Jam from Hard Fruit.
When making jam from hard fruit, cook the fruit by itself with just the water that remains from washing, until it is easy to remove the stones. Then add the sugar and continue the cooking until the jam will set. Cool the jam slightly, then pot.

The right proportion of sugar is another essential in successful jam-making, and the following is generally accepted:-
Hard fruits: 1 lb. sugar to 1 lb. of fruit.
Soft fruit: 3/4 lb. sugar to 1 lb. of fruit.

Potting and Storing.
The jars used must be sterilized. Wash them thoroughly and rinse in clean water. Then put them into a saucepan of water, bring them to the boil, and leave them in the hot water until ready to be used. They need not then be dried. Pour the jam or jelly into the pots, making them quire full, and allow it to cool and set before covering.

Then wipe the outside and rim of the pots until quite free from all stickiness, and cover the contents with a thin layer of melted paraffin wax.

This can be bought in small cakes or slabs. The quantity required should be melted in a small saucepan. Pour a little on to each pot with a spoon and see that the inner side of the rim is completely covered. Allow the wax to harden before putting on the top cover. If unable to obtain the paraffin wax, use rounds of paper dipped in vinegar. For the top covers, if screw tops are not available, use vegetable parchment paper. Label the jars at the side, putting on the date when made as well as the kind. Store all jams and jellies in a perfectly dry, airy cupboard.

Mint Sauce

1/4 pint vinegar

1/8 pint boiling water

1 teaspoon sugar

2 tablespoon chopped mint

Add the sugar tae the boiling water. Add it tae the vinegar, and when cold, pour a' over the chopped mint. Stand aside for an hour and use as required.

151

Blackberry Wine
Cover fruit with water. Stand 48 hrs. Bring to boiling pt & strain
To each quart of liquid add 1 lb of sugar a little each day for 7 days stirring often. Bottle but do not screw corks down for some time

BOTTLING FRUITS

The apparatus required is not elaborate. A large boiling-pan for heating the water will do in place of a proper sterilizer, a thermometer, and a supply of fruit-bottling jars, preferably with glass or porcelain-lined lids. (Otherwise, lids must be lined with wax paper.) These have screw tops, and are fitted with rubber bands. Particular attention should be paid to the lids and jars, to ascertain they are free from cracks, and that the rubber bands fit properly. If there are any chips or the lids dinna screw on tightly, air will enter. Always buy new rubber rings for each year's bottling. It is false economy to use the old, which may have stretched or perished.

Preparing the Fruit.
Choose fruit that is slightly under-ripe. It must be unblemished, without bruises or broken skin, and should be graded so that the fruit of equal size is bottled together. The method of preparation varies according to the fruit, after, of course, it has been cleansed.

Peaches and Nectarines. Drop into boiling water, leave for 2 minutes, then peel. Cut in half with a silver knife, remove stones, and pack the fruit in the bottles with the cut side downwards.
Apples and Pears. Peel and quarter.
Gooseberries. Top and tail.
Currants. Take lightly from their stalks by drawing the prongs of a fork through them.
Large Plums. Cut in half, and stone.
Raspberries, Blackberries, Loganberries. These must not be washed, but they should be picked over, and a special look-out kept for the tiny white caterpillars which are not infrequently found in fine specimens of this fruit.

Pack the fruit to within half an inch of the top of the bottles. A little care taken in packing the bottles does much to enhance the finished appearance. A long spoon or a clean, smooth piece of wood is useful when filling. Great care should be taken not to crush the fruit. Fill the bottles with cold water to overflowing, and screw up partly so that the air may escape during the sterilization process.

Place the bottles in a sterilizer, fish kettle, boiler, or bath, containing sufficient cold water to reach almost to the neck of the bottles. Most sterilizers are provided with a tray on which the bottles rest, but when using an improvised one, such as a bath or boiler, it is essential to provide a false bottom. Wood is a poor conductor of heat, so that a bottom made of wooden slats answers excellently. Otherwise, there is always the chance that the heat passing directly from the metal to the thick glass bottle will cause it to crack. For a fish kettle, brown paper may be utilized. Several thicknesses should be placed in the bottom of the pan, and kept in position with the strainer, on which the bottles should stand; this arrangement facilitates the removal of the bottles when sterilization is completed. If preferred, a folded cloth may be substituted for the brown paper.

Begin to heat the water in the sterilizer over a slow fire or low gas-jet. The temperature of the water must be raised to 180° F., or simmering point, and the bottles allowed to remain in the water at this temperature for 15 minutes before, fruit is sterilized. The process takes between 1 1/2 and 1 3/4 hours. An inexperienced person should rely on a thermometer, but it is quite possible to bottle fruit without one, for simmering point is reached when small bubbles arise at the sides of the pan and break quietly on the surface of the water. These small bubbles must not be confused with the large bubbles which burst with vigour when boiling point, 212° F., is reached.

When the Fruit is Sterilized.
Lift the jars from the water and place them on a wooden table or newspaper. If you put a hot glass bottle on to cold metal it is liable to crack. Complete the crewing-down of the metal tops and leave to cool. Next day remove the metal top and life the bottle by the glass lid, which is possible if the bottle is airtight.

Store in a cool, dry cupboard and inspect each bottle carefully at the end of 8 days. If there are signs of fermentation, the fruit must either be re-sterilized or used at once.

If ordinary jam jars, or fruit bottles without special lids, are used, the process is exactly similar to that described, except that the jars are open during sterilization, and that perfectly clean melted mutton fat is poured into the bottle immediately after it is removed from the sterilizer. The bottles must then be covered with bladder or parchment paper. Soak the bladder in warm water, dry in a cloth to remove the surplus moisture, stretch it tightly over the top of the bottle, and tie down.

152

Apple Sauce

4 guid-sized apples

1 tbs water

1 oz. butter

2 tbs moist sugar

A squeeze lemon juice

Pare, core, and quarter the apples. Put them in a stewpan wi' the cold water and twa tablespoonfuls moist sugar. Simmer a' thegither till the apples are a pulp; add a docl o' butter. If the apples are awfy juicy, ye'll need tae boil it awfy quickly, stirring well for five or six minutes tae reduce the liquid. Add lemon juice and beat well till smooth.

Horse-radish Sauce

1 horse-radish
1/2 tsp mustard
1 tsp caster sugar
2 raw egg yolks
Pinch salt
About 1 gill stiffly-
whisked cream
1 1/2 tbsps vinegar

Let the horse-radish
lie in water till
firm. Scrub well.
Peel and grate
finely. Take the
mustard, caster
sugar, raw yolks
of eggs, and the
salt, and mix well.
Gradually add the
cream and vinegar.
Lastly, the horse-
radish.

A QUICK WAY OF MAKING PICCALILLI

1 cucumber
1/2 oz. turmeric
1 cauliflower
1/2 oz. curry powder
1 lb. small onions
2 ozs. Mustard
1 marrow
1 oz. sugar
2 tablespoonfuls cornflour

Cut the marrow into small pieces, strip the cauliflower, peel the onions, cut the cucumber into small cubes, and lay all in salt for 12 hours. Then drain well, and put into a large pan with 2 quarts of vinegar, and bring to a boil. Mix the turmeric, curry, mustard, sugar and cornflour with a little cold vinegar, and add to the boiling liquor. Boil all for 5 minutes, stirring well.

Raspberry Jam

4 lb Scottish raspberries

4 lb sugar

Add the fruit tae a jelly pan and warm on a low heat until the juice starts tae run. Add the sugar tae the fruit and stir until it dissolves. Bring tae the boil and test regularly tae see if it has set. You can test tae see if it's set by drapping a wee drap o' jam onto a plate. Wait for a few seconds, then draw your finger across the surface of the jam and if it wrinkles then the jam has reached its setting point. Warm some jeely jars in the oven. Ye hae tae be careful daein' this. Let the mixture cool for around 15 minutes. Pot the jam in the warm jars. Serve with fresh scones or Scotch pancakes.

Tomato Chutney

8 pints green tomatoes
6 large onions
1 cup salt
8 cups water
4 cups vinegar
2 lbs. brown sugar
1/4 lb. mustard seeds
2 tbsps. cinnamon
2 tbsps. allspice
2 tbsps. cloves
2 tbsps. ginger
1 tsp. cayenne pepper

Slice the onions and green tomatoes. Sprinkle them with salt, and leave to stand overnight. Drain the liquor off. Boil the sugar and vinegar with the spices (in a muslin bag if you wish). Put the tomatoes and onions in a large pot. Boil for 15 minutes and then drain. Cover with the vinegar and spices, boil for another 15 minutes.

E HOUSEWIFE.

Chutneys and Pickles.

Date Chutney.

3lbs. of pressed dates.
1 pint of vinegar, or more if liked.
1oz. of all kinds of spice, mace, clove, pepper, etc.

Method.—Stone and prepare dates and press into glass jam jars. Boil the spice in the vinegar and pour on to dates while hot, tie down, and allow to stand a week or so, when it will be ready for use.—*H. E. Collinson, Las Flores, The Knoll, Beckenham.*

Clear Cucumber Pickle.

Peel and cut into cubes any quantity of green cucumbers, and leave to soak twenty-four hours in salt and water, then strain away brine. Make a pickle in proportion of 1½lbs. of sugar, one level tablespoonful each of whole spice, peppercorns, and cloves to one quart of vinegar. When this is boiling, add cucumbers and boil until they are clear.—*Miss Powell, Vron, Meliden Road, Prestatyn, N.W.*

Sweet Fruit Pickle.

This can be made with the dried fruits salad, such as figs, peaches, and apricots.

Steep one pound of the dried fruits for twenty-four hours, then boil one pound of yellow sugar with half a pint of vinegar until it becomes thick. Add one tablespoonful each of ground mace and allspice. Mix all the ingredients together and simmer gently in an enamel pan for one hour. Bottle and seal tightly when cold.—*Mrs. Lester, 210, Birdholme, Chesterfield.*

To Pickle Mushrooms.

Choose small, white mushrooms of one night's growth. Cut off roots and rub the top of mushrooms with a piece of flannel dipped in salt. Put them in a stew jar, allowing to every quart of mushrooms one ounce each of salt and ginger, half an ounce of whole pepper, eight blades of mace, a bay leaf, a strip of lemon rind, and a wineglassful of cooking sherry. Cover the jar close and let it stand on the hob or stove so as to be thoroughly heated and on boiling point. Let it be a day or so until the liquid is absorbed, then cover with hot vinegar, close it again and stand until it just boils, then take from the fire. When cold put into wide-mouthed bottles and tie down. In a week's time add more vinegar if required. Cork tightly and dip in bottle resin.—*Mrs. M. Baxter, 4, Sidney Terrace, Stamfordham, Newcastle.*

Pear Chutney.

2lbs. ripe pears, weighed after being peeled and cored.
6ozs. of brown sugar.
2 large apples (rather acid).
1 large Spanish onion, chopped **fine**.
4ozs. seedless raisins.
1 stick of cinnamon.
A small piece of root ginger.
1 pint of vinegar.

Boil the pears until quite soft, then add one tablespoonful of salt, one teaspoonful each ground ginger and whole cloves, saltspoonful each spice and pepper. Boil quarter of an hour, then remove ginger and cinnamon. Bottle when cold. Cover.—*Mrs. Taylor, 7, Richard Street, Leicester.*

Hasty Mint Chutney.

Take a handful of fresh mint, another handful of sultanas (cleaned, stoned, and sliced), also two tablespoonfuls of sugar and a little cayenne pepper or a chilli (dried), and a saltspoonful of salt. Pound all these ingredients in a mortar till they are juicy and soft and add two tablespoonfuls of vinegar. No cooking is required.—*Miss P. Boughtflower, c/o Mrs. Brett, Lavington, 14, Shirley Road, Croydon.*

A Cheap and Delicious Pickle.

Take some Spanish onions, cut them into rings, put into a jar with some old peppers, a few cloves to taste, and two tablespoonfuls of white sugar. Pour on cold vinegar. Tie down; ready in a week. Lovely with cold meats.—*Mrs. Richards, 157, Garratt Lane, Wandsworth, S.W.10.*

Rhubarb and Ginger Jam

This is my favourite jam. It is jist delicious on scones. Tae be honest, it is braw wi' onything. My laddie takes it on his porridge.

7 lb rhubarb

7 lb sugar

1 lemon

2 lb crystallised ginger

Wash the rhubarb and cut into small pieces. Put this in alternate layers with the sugar into a large earthenware pot. Squeeze the lemon and pour the juice into the pot and leave this overnight. The next day there should be a guid amount of liquid that has seeped fae the rhubarb. Drain this aff into a jelly pan and boil it with the preserved ginger for around 15 minutes. Then add the rhubarb and boil for a further fifteen minutes. After this time remove fae the heat, skim any scum fae the surface of the pot and after around 15 minutes cooling time pour into pots warmed in the oven or wi" biled water.

Orange Marmalade

5 lbs oranges

8 pints of water

7 lb sugar

Wash the fruit. Put it in a very large pot. Add 8 pints of water and bring tae the boil, cover, then simmer for around 1 hour or till the fruit is soft. Drain the oranges but dinna throw awa' the liquid. Let the oranges cool and then cut them into quarters. Scoop out the flesh, and set aside. Remove the pips (put the pips aside for later too). Take the orange skins and remove as much pith as you can, but keep this too. Put the pips and pith into a small pan and simmer in ½ pint of water for about 20 minutes. This liquid is vital tae set the marmalade. Strain it and set aside. Cut the orange peel finely. Grease a jelly pan. Add all the reserved ingredients to a large measuring jug, and for every 1 pint add 1 lb of sugar. Add liquid and sugar tae the pan ower a low heat. When sugar has melted, bring the mixture tae the boil. Boil and stir continuously. After around 20 minutes, test and pour into dry warm jars.

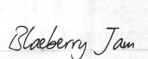

The straining of fruit for jelly-making is a long and tedious process, but the accompanying illustration shows an easy method of accomplishing the task.

The flannel is fashioned into a tapering bag. Strong tape is securely fixed at the corners and tied to the chairs. The bowl is placed on the floor between. Something heavy is placed on the seat of each chair to prevent the weight of the bag tipping them up.

The fruit is left to strain overnight.

...ans foul drains.

Blæberry Jam

7 lbs. blueberries
1 lb. thin red rhubarb
5 lbs. sugar

Pick over the berries and remove any scraps of leaf or stem. Wipe the rhubarb and cut into inch-lengths.

Put it into the preserving-pan with the sugar, heat slowly, and boil for 10 minutes. Add the blueberries and simmer, skimming well, until the fruit is tender. Test, and when sufficiently set, pour into dry, warm jars. Cover when cold.

Rose-Hip Jelly

Rose-Hips
Sugar
Crab Apples
Butter

Use the bright scarlet hips of the wild rose for this jelly, to every breakfastcupful of hips, denuded of their seeds, allow one pound of crab apples. Wash these, and cut into quarters without peeling or coring. Put them in a pan with the hips and water to cover, and simmer till quite soft. Strain through a flannel jelly-bag, but dinna squeeze the fruit.

Butter your pan lightly with unsalted butter, pour in the juice, allowing to each pint 1 lb. of the best preserving-sugar. Boil the syrup for 10 minutes, or until it jells when tested. Pour into warmed jars, and cover when cold.
This jelly is a lovely rose-colour, and has tonic qualities.
Rose hips should never be cooked in an aluminium pan.
Enamel is best.

Apple Jelly

Add 1 lb of preserving sugar, and the rind of one lemon to each pint of apple juice. It's Aipple Jeely we really ca' it.

Apple juice
Sugar and lemons according tae quantity

Wash and cut up the apples into pieces, but neither pare nor core. Place in preserving-pan with sufficient water tae cover. Bring tae boil, and continue tae boil gently till the fruit is a pulp. Stir at intervals with a wooden spoon. Pour into jelly bag tae drip a' night. The resulting juice should be thick when cold. Measure, and place in preserving-pan with the juice and lemon rind. Tie up the lemon-rind in a small piece of muslin. Bring tae the boil, then add sufficient sugar. Stir continuously till the sugar melts, then boil rapidly. The jelly is done when a wee drap wrinkles on a cold plate. The time taken should be between 20 minutes and 1/2 hour. Remove rind, skim, and pot. Ye really shouldna mak' a lot o' aipple jeely at once as it will no' keep.

Redcurrant Jelly

4 lbs. redcurrants
Sugar according to juice

Clean and pick currants. Place them in a large earthenware container and add a 1/4 pint of water and 1/4 lb. of granulated sugar. Place a saucer over the top of the jar, stand in a large pan of water, and place at the side of the stove so that it cooks gently. When all the juice is extracted from the fruit, pour it off and drain through a jelly bag. When strained, place in a preserving-pan with 1 3/4 lbs. of loaf sugar to each quart of juice. Boil, keeping it well stirred and skimmed. Test in the usual way on a plate. Allow to cool, then pour into dry pots and tie tops on. This jelly is for serving with mutton.

Blackberry Jelly

Again, allow 1 lb of preserving sugar tae every pint of juice frae the fruit.

6 lbs. blackberries
2 lbs. cooking apples
Water, enough to cover fruit
Sugar according tae quantity of juice

Wipe apples clean, and cut up, but dinna peel or core, and boil them with the blackberries until soft, just covering them with water. Put in a straining cloth or jelly bag, and set aside for the night. Squeeze gently tae mak' sure ye get a' the juice, and add preserving sugar; boil till it sets on a cold plate. Put in small jars, cover and tie.

Granpaw's Special Pickled Onions

Choose small fresh silver onions, and place them in salt and water for a few hours. Peel till the onions have a clear attractive appearance, but dinna cut them in any way. Boil up some spiced white vinegar. This is prepared by adding a 1/4 oz. of allspice, 1/2 oz. of white peppercorns, 2 cloves and 1 teaspoonful of salt to each pint of vinegar. After skimming place the onions in this and allow to simmer gently for 5 minutes. Pour into jars and tie down.

Paw's Pickled Gherkins

Make up some salt water, and leave the gherkins to soak in it for fower or five days. Dry, and put them in jars that have been sterilised in a hot oven. Prepare enough vinegar to cover by adding to each quart 1/2 oz. of ginger and 1 oz. of allspice. Boil this up for 10 minutes, pour it over the gherkins, and cover each jar wi' a saucer. Leave them somewhere warm overnight. Next morning, pour off the vinegar into a pot. Boil it again, and again pour it over the gherkins. Put on lids or tie down the jars with circles of greased paper when they are cold, and keep for 6 weeks.

Chutney

There's mair ingredients than there's method for this, but oh! it's rare and tasty.

1/4 lb. preserved ginger	1 lb. sultanas
2 1/2 ozs. garlic	1 1/2 quarts malt vinegar
1 oz. mustard seeds	2 dozen apples or more
2 lbs. sugar	6 sliced figs
1/2 lb. salt	1 oz. citron (cut fine)
1/4 lb. onions	1/2 teaspoon horse radish
1/2 lb. seedless raisins	

Chop garlic and onions and raisins till it looks like mince. Chop a' thegither. Add all ingredients to a large pot and boil slowly for 40 minutes. Stir occasionally. Bottle and cork well.

Weel, Maggie, that's a' frae me. I'm sure ye'll manage tae fill a' the blank pages I've left ye. And aye remember, if onybody tells ye that wummin's place is in the kitchen, just gie them an apron and a bang on the lug!

Brown Sauce

1 oz. butter
1 oz. flour
1/2 pint stock
1 small onion
1 small tomato
One small carrot
Salt and pepper

Melt the butter, and fry
the onion till it is brown.
Add the flour and fry
together till it takes on a
brown colour. Add the stock,
vegetables and seasoning.
Boil, then turn down and
simmer a half hour; strain.
Serve with meats.

Maw's Favourites

maw Is
The besT
aT cookin

Tattie and Mutton Soup

1 neck of mutton
1.2 litres/ 2 pints water
salt and pepper
A bay leaf
1 kg/ 2g lb peeled potatoes
1 large onion
3 to 4 carrots, peeled and thinly
sliced or grated
Chopped chives or parsley

Bring the neck of mutton to the boil and then simmer for around 30 minutes. Remove any scum from the surface of the pot. Chop the vegetables finely and add them to the pot with some salt and pepper and the bay leaf. Cover the pot and cook for around 30 minutes until the vegetables are tender. Remove the bay leaf. Remove the meat from the pan, slice finely and then return to the pot. Taste the soup and add more seasoning if necessary. Just before serving, add the parsley.

Free

The Beautiful 'OXO' Doll for 480

OXO Cube Outside Wrappers

You can obtain this ovely gift **at once.** All you have to do is to send to OXO Ltd. the requisite number of OXO Cube Outside Wrappers.

Look in the Shop Windows

"Little Betty OXO"
(17 ins. high)

TOMATO PIE

4 small Tomatoes
1/2 lb. cold Boiled Beef
1 Egg
Parsley
Pepper and 1/2 gill Stock made by adding 1 teaspoonful Bisto to teacupful Water

Cut tomatoes into slices, and **beef into** neat, small pieces, removing skin and gristle. Arrange in alternate layers and pour over beaten egg, mixed with stock, like custard (not too full). Dish is lined round sides with pastry, edges being well covered, and strips of paste arranged diagonally over top. Then cover edge all round and mark neatly. Glaze with egg or milk and bake 3/4 hour.

STEWED SAUSAGES

1 lb. Sausages
1 oz. Fat
Boiling Water or Stock
1 teasp. Bisto or Browned Flour

Method:
1. Scald sausages, then brown well in smoking hot fat.
2. Pour off fat and add water or stock. Simmer 1/2 hour.
3. Thicken gravy as for brown stew.

Harvest Broth

680 g/1 1/2 lb neck of lamb
225 g/8 oz shelled peas
450 g/4 oz shelled broad beans with
casing removed
8 spring onions finely chopped
2 carrots
1/2 turnip chopped
1 small curly kail cabbage
Salt
2.4 litres/ 4 pints water
2 tablespoons chopped parsley

Chop the neck of lamb and trim off the fat. Add the meat to the pan with the water and some salt. Bring the liquid to the boil and skim the surface of fat and other residues. Add the carrots, turnip, peas, beans and onions and boil for an hour. After an hour, add the chopped curly kail and boil for a further 30 minutes. After this, add the chopped parsley and serve. Serves six to eight.

USEFUL HINTS ON BATTER

Careful Mixing is the Secret of Success

THERE is no culinary matter on which women are more divided in opinion than that of batter. The pancake is a simple sweet, but it would seem that no two batches of pancakes present the same appearance and flavour. It is the same with that much-discussed dainty, Yorkshire pudding. I have known people grow quite virulent about that; and once, when a mere man broke into print, and gave a curious and somewhat complicated recipe for "Yorkshire," he drew the fury and contempt of women cooks from Land's End to John o' Groats.

The success of batter is more a question of discretion in mixing than of quantities of material. Roughly speaking, the proportions are: Half a pound of flour to one pint of milk and two eggs. Flour should be plain and not self-raising, and I have discovered that the best results are obtained when a mixture of a third of water to two-thirds of milk are used. This helps to make the batter lighter.

METHOD OF MIXING

Put the flour in a basin, with a liberal pinch of salt. Toss the flour lightly with the fingers, unless you have previously sifted it. Then make a hole in the centre, and drop in the eggs, whole, one at a time, working the mixture with a wooden spoon until smooth, add milk, and more flour if necessary, to make it to the consistency of thick cream. Beat well, taking care that it is perfectly smooth. Put aside for at least two hours; more if you can.

regulate oven, this difficulty is disposed of, for the meat can be shifted to the lower, or cool, shelf, and the pudding go into the top, or hot, shelf.

A GOOD HINT

However, as the pudding, poured into a small baking dish of boiling fat, requires only ten minutes of a really hot oven in order to "rise," it is possible to risk placing the meat on the lower shelf for that time, covering it with another pan to prevent it from hardening. After that, lower the heat of the oven, and leave the pudding to cook with the meat. The heat of the dripping into which the pudding is poured makes all the difference between crisp edges and "soggy" ones. And it must be remembered that the proof of the pudding is not, in this case, the eating, but the cooking! But no two housewives will ever agree on this matter of Yorkshire pudding.

Some Recipes Tested by Our Specialist

can make a baked batter pudding in the same way, only flavouring with sugar, baking it in a well-buttered pie dish, and serving it with jam or jam sauce.

Now that eggs are cheaper, I can dare to give you recipes that require more than one or two. Here is a waffle mixture that may please you.

WAFFLES

Required: ½lb. of flour, three teaspoonfuls of baking powder, 3 eggs, half a pint of milk, salt to taste, and 2 tablespoonfuls of melted butter.

Mix the flour and baking powder, and work in gradually, the egg yolks and the milk, beat to a stiff cream. Then add the melted butter, and lastly, the stiffly beaten whites of the eggs. Cream well. Grease the waffle iron with good dripping; pour in some of the batter, and close the iron. Cook over a clear fire for about two minutes, turn the iron, and cook the other side. Open the iron, remove the waffle, and serve with either butter and brown sugar, maple or golden syrup—a good breakfast dish.

FRYING BATTER

This batter, in which you may cook fish, meat, or fruit, is best made with oil. The proportions are four tablespoonfuls of flour, half a teaspoonful of salt, a quarter pint of tepid water, white of half an egg, half a tablespoonful of salad oil.

Make a batter, like thick cream, with flour, oil, and tepid water. Just before using stir in the white of egg, stiffly beaten. You may make fritters of any kind of fruit, fresh or tinned, by dipping in this batter, and frying crisp in deep boiling fat. When the fritters are plunged into boiling

Treacle Toffee

5 tablesp. sugar
2½ ozs. butter
1 tablesp. syrup, treacle
milk & water.
½ teasp. honey

Lentil soup

100g /4 oz lentils
25 g/1 oz vegetable oil
75g /3 oz carrots
50 g/2 oz ~~Swe~~ turnips
1 onion
1 large potato
1 litre/2 pints water
1 ham hough
Black pepper

Add the water to the pot and the ham hough and bring tae the boil. Simmer for around 2 hours, after which you should remove the ham hough, strain and reserve the stock, and skim off any fat. Wash the lentils and dice the vegetables. Pour a little vegetable oil into a large pot and cook the vegetables over a low heat with the lid on for around 20 minutes. Add the lentils and the stock and simmer for about 2 hours. Shred the meat from the ham hough and add to the soup. Taste and season.

Easy Haggis

200 g/8 oz sheep's liver
100 g/4 oz beef suet
2 large onions
100 g/4 oz ~~fine~~ toasted oatmeal
Salt and pepper

Boil the liver in a pan of water for around 40 minutes. Retain this water once the liver is cooked, remove the liver. and mince it finely. Cook the onions on a low heat in a frying pan with a little suet. Chop them finely with the rest of the suet. Toast the oatmeal. Combine a' the ingredients in a bowl and season with salt and pepper. Moisten the mixture using the liquid in which the liver was cooked. Press the mixture into a pudding basin, cover the top with foil and tie in place, and place in a large pot of water, and boil for 2 hours.
Serve with mashed potato, mashed neep and butter, or with clapshot.

DATE AND WALNUT LOAF

1 cup boiling water
250 g/8 oz stoned dates
2 level tsps bicarbonate of soda
1 pinch of salt
125 g/4 oz sugar
125 g/4 oz butter
1 egg
425 g/14 oz plain flour
50 g/2 oz chopped walnuts
1 tsp vanilla extract

Set the oven to 180°C/350°F/ gas mark 4. Pour the boiling water over the dates and add the bicarbonate of soda. Leave this to stand while you cream together the butter and sugar. Whisk the eggs. Then sieve the flour and add the salt to it. Fold in alternate spoonfuls of beaten egg and flour into the creamed butter and sugar until smooth. Mix the dates and the water in with the mixture and add the vanilla. Grease a 20-cm/8-inch loaf tin. Pour the mixture into the tin and then place on the middle shelf of the oven for an hour. When cooled slice and spread with butter.

Clootie Dumpling

A tasty, filling pudding speckled with a generous helping of fruit

125 g/4 oz suet, chopped
250 g/8 oz self-raising flour
1 tsp baking powder
125 g/4 oz breadcrumbs
75 g/3 oz brown sugar
1 grated apple
200 g/8 oz currants and sultanas, or mixed fruit
1 tsp cinnamon, ginger, nutmeg
1 tbsp golden syrup
2 eggs

Half fill a very large pot and bring to the boil. Scald a large piece of linen or cheesecloth with boiling water then dust it with flour. Beat the eggs, mix in the syrup and a little milk, and gradually mix into the dry ingredients and fruit. Place the mixture in the middle of the cloth. Tie securely but allow for swelling. Place an inverted plate on the bottom of the pan and put the pudding on it. Boil for 3–4 hours. Keep checking the pan and never allow the water to drop below half the depth of the pudding. When it is ready, dip in cold water, remove the cloth and dry the pudding off in the oven. Serve with cream or custard.

Housewife Weekly "cut out and keep" **Scottish Recipes** No.3

cut here

Mocha Cake. (Mrs Knowles.)

9 ozs. Butter, 9 ozs. Sugar, 9 ozs Flour,
4 eggs, 1 teaspoon Bak. Powder,
2 dessertspoon; Coffee Essence.
Beat the butter & sugar together till creamy, beat up the eggs & add coffee essence to them, place bak. Powder to the flour, then sift in a little of the flour and egg alternately, put in a greased tin lined with paper & hollow out the centre & bake in a moderate oven ¾ of an hour. (If desired brown add a little Bi carbonate of soda.)
Butter icing for same
1 oz butter 2 ozs icing sugar. & beat well together add just a little coffee essence.

Smiddy Dumpling

This recipe is Jean Thomson's. It is a far easier way of making dumpling than Granmaw's recipe!

1 cup sugar
2 cups sultanas
4 oz/100 g butter
1 cup water
1 teaspoon baking soda
1 teaspoon mixed spice

Bring all of the ingredients to the boil in a heavy bottomed pot for around two minutes. When this mixture is cool add:

1 cup plain flour
1 cup self raising flour
2 eggs, beaten

Combine all the ingredients well and place in a large, buttered, round cake tin. Cook for 1 1/2 hours at 150°C/300°F.

Cheese Dishes

Batter for crêpes (12)
4 oz flour
1 large egg
½ pt milk   ½ teas. butter
Frying pan about 6" diameter
Thin layer of batter for each crêpe.

Fondue for filling
4 fluid oz fairly dry white wine
8 oz Lancashire cheese   2 teas cornflour
melt together in saucepan
over low heat.
Add small measure of kirsch
Season with pepper.

Hollandaise sauce.
½ pt milk.
1 oz flour
1 oz butter
2 egg yolks
3 teas. lemon juice, salt + pepper
In saucepan make flour milk +
egg yolks. Stir well over
gentle heat. Add lemon salt +
pepper

...was remitted for trial to the High Co...
...Perth on 19th January.

As a
NIGHT-
CAP

It induces sleep,
It soothes and warms,
And guards us 'gainst
Chill winter's harms

VAN
HOUTEN'S
COCOA

Best & Goes Farthest.

COCOA

One teaspoonful of cocoa to a **breakfast cup**. Sugar to sweeten. **Half breakfast cup** milk and half breakfast cup water.

Mix **the** sugar with the cocoa. **Put** the milk and water on to heat, and when **it** boils, pour it on to the cocoa, stirring all **the** time. Return to the pan and boil. Then serve.

A BREAKFAST-TABLE BAROMETER

A cup of hot coffee is an unfailing **barometer**, if you allow a lu**mp of su**gar to drop to the bottom **of** the cup and watch the air bubbles **arise** without disturbing the coffee.

If the bubbles collect in the middle, the weather will be fine; if they **adhere** to the cup, forming a **ring**, it will either **rain** or **snow**; and if the bubbles **separate** without assuming **any** fixed position, changeable weather may be expected.

TELEPHONE MESSAGE

Date.................... Time..............

To ....

From ....

Phone Number ....

Mix in   thick cream.

Fill each crêpe with fondue,
roll up + put in fairly hot oven for
about 10 minutes
Pour the Hollandaise sauce
over the pannequets, place
under hot grill for few
minutes

Coffee
3 heaped tablespoons coffee
1 pint boiling water
allow to stand for 2 minutes
remove coffee ground by passing
spoon over top of liquid in jug

Signature....................

Paris Buns.

{ 1 Oven
{ 2 Prepare Tin }
¼ lb of Flour.
1 oz of butter.
1 oz castor sugar.
½ teasp. cream of tarter.
¼ teas. bi-carb. of soda
grated lemon rind (or lemon essence
squeeze of juice)
½ egg.
¼ teacupful sweet milk.
Note. 1 oz currants or sultanas may be added
for seed buns 1 teas. Caraway Buns.

Empire Biscuits

This recipe is Barbara Browning's. Her empire biscuits are definitely the best.

75 g/3 oz butter
25 g/1 oz sugar
100 g/4 oz self-raising flour
Raspberry jam or jelly
150 g/6 oz icing sugar
Approx. 2 tsps water
Lemon juice

Cream the butter and sugar together. Sieve the flour and mix into the butter. Roll out thinly (about 3 or 4 mm/1/8 inch) and cut into rounds. Bake on the middle shelf for 10 minutes 180°C/355°F/ gas mark 4, or until golden. Cool and spread half of the biscuits with jam on their rough sides. Sandwich the biscuits together in pairs. Mix up the icing sugar, water and lemon juice and coat the top of each biscuit. Leave to set.

Caramel Shortbread

Make shortbread (your usual recipe)
1 large tin condensed milk (400 g/14 oz)
200g/ 7 oz 70% cocoa chocolate, or any good quality milk
  chocolate

The day before you make the shortbread, place a tin of condensed milk, pierced at the top, in a pan of water, bring to the boil and then simmer over a medium heat for two hours. Remove from the heat and leave overnight.

Make the shortbread, your usual way, in a shallow tin. Allow to cool. Spread caramelised condensed milk over the shortbread once cooled. Melt the chocolate and spread over the caramel. Slice before it is completely cool, then leave in a cool place for the toppings to set.

Pitcaithly Bannocks

150 g/6 oz plain flour
25 g/1 oz cornflour
75 g/3 oz caster sugar
100 g/4 oz butter
40 g/1 1/2 oz preserved peel
40 g/1 1/2 oz blanched almonds
40 g/1 1/2 oz orange peel

Sieve the flour. Cream the butter and sugar together and gradually mix it with the flour. Chop the almonds and the peel very finely. Mix these ingredients with the shortbread dough. Roll the dough into a round that is about 20 cm/8 inches in diameter and score into eight segments. Prick the surface with a fork. Bake on a baking sheet at 150 C/300 F/gas mark 2 for around 50 minutes or until the shortbread turns golden but not brown. Transfer to a wire cooling tray and sprinkle with caster sugar.

Shortbread

500 g/1 lb butter, softened
175 g/7 oz caster sugar
600 g/1 1/4 lb plain flour, sieved
(crunchier biscuits can be made by
substituting 50 g /2 oz semolina for 50 g
/2 oz plain flour)

Preheat the oven to 160°C/325°F/gas mark
3. Beat together the butter and the
sugar. Beat in the flour and semolina,
100 g/4 oz at a time, until smooth.
If the dough becomes too stiff to stir,
knead in the rest of the flour with your
hands. Grease and flour a large baking
tray. Roll out the dough and press into
the baking sheet. Mark the dough into
fingers or pie-shaped wedges and prick
the pieces all over with the prongs of a
fork. Bake in the centre of the oven for
30 to 40 minutes or until firm tae the
touch. Makes about two dozen biscuits.

Perfect for kids' summer parties, these swee...

Marshmallow party buns

1 pack ready-to-roll fondant icing
Food colouring
1 pack fairy cakes or sweet buns
Apricot jam
Princess Marshmallows
4 tbsp icing sugar
Sweets and sugar decorations

Make up different colours of fondant by kneading in a little food colouring. Roll out fondant and cut into circles big enough to cover cake tops. Use jam to stick icing to cakes.

Mix a little water into icing sugar to make a smooth paste. Add food colouring as required and use to fill a piping bag.

Use icing to stick sweets, decorations and Princess Marshmallows on to cakes and add eyes, smiles, swirls or whatever else you'd like.

Tablet - A rich, sweet treat

200 g/8 oz condensed milk
50 g/2 oz butter
1 kg/2 lb sugar
1 cup milk
Vanilla essence (optional)

Bring the ingredients to the boil slowly in a large thick-bottomed saucepan and stir regularly. After a few minutes, test consistency by dropping a little of the mixture into cold water (it should be like soft putty), or use a sugar thermometer and stop heating when it reaches 240°F/108°C (soft ball). Remove from the heat and beat with a wooden spoon until the mixture begins to solidify. Pour into a greased tray and cut into bars.

cut here

Housewife Weekly
"cut out and keep"
Scottish Recipes

No.25

Peppermint Creams

Whites of two medium eggs
200 g/8 oz icing sugar
Peppermint oil

Beat the eggs with a hand mixer and add the sieved icing sugar gradually also using a hand blender until the paste becomes too difficult for the mixer tae mix. Make a well in the middle of the paste and drop in around three drops of peppermint oil. Knead this in with your hands. Knead in the rest of the icing sugar. Taste the paste and add more peppermint if required and knead through.
Roll out to around ½ cm/¼ inch thick and cut out round shapes with a cutter, alternatively pinch off small balls of the mixture and flatten them. Place in a cool place tae harden and store in an airtight tin.

BURNT CREAM
OR CRÈME BRULÉE

500 ml/1 pint double cream
4 egg yolks
3 level tbsps caster sugar
2 drops vanilla extract, or one vanilla pod halved,
with seeds scraped off and added to the pan
Caster or brown sugar for the top of the custard

Preheat the oven to 180°C/350°F/gas mark 4. Add the cream, and vanilla pod if you're using it, to a saucepan and very slowly bring to just below boiling point. Beat the eggs yolks together with the 3 tbsps caster sugar in a large bowl. To this bowl you gradually beat in the almost boiling cream (not the other way round) and then, when thoroughly beaten together, return the mixture to the saucepan.

Cook on a low heat, taking care not to boil it, for around 5 to 10 minutes, stirring continuously. Add the vanilla extract if you're using it, or remove the vanilla pod at this stage if that was your choice to flavour the custard.

Pour the custard into an ovenproof dish. Fill a roasting tray half full with boiling water. I find it is easiest and safest to open the oven that has been preheating, pull out a shelf in the middle, place the roasting pan on the shelf and pour in the boiling water from the kettle as it sits on the shelf. Then place the dish in the hot water on the tray. Cook the custard until it has lightly set which should be around 40 minutes, but check the consistency by tapping it with a spoon or a finger.

Leave this to cool and then chill in the refrigerator overnight. The next day sprinkle with caster or brown sugar and caramelise either using a chef's blow torch or under the grill. Chill again so that the caramelised sugar is crunchy.

Serve with Scottish raspberries. This dish can also be made in individual ramekin dishes but remember to reduce the cooking time a little.

Macaroon Bars

2 large floury potatoes, cooked and mashed till smooth
Approx 300 g/9 oz icing sugar
1 small drop glycerine
Melted chocolate for coating
Toasted dessicated coconut

Boil two potatoes for 20 minutes and then mash very smoothly indeed. Using a food mixer, mix in a little icing sugar at a time, and add one drop of glycerine, until it turns into a firm dough. Pinch off a piece of the dough and taste to ensure that you have included enough sugar. It should not taste of potato. If it does, add a spoonful of water and more icing sugar. Press into a tray and cut into bars. When set firmly, coat the bars in melted chocolate and then dip in toasted dessicated coconut.

My favourite!!!

Isa and Jimmy Brownlee's recipe.

Tablet

125 g/4 oz salted butter (butter with
   strong flavour is best)
1 kg/ 2 1/4 lb granulated sugar
1 cup full-cream milk
400 g/14 oz tin of condensed milk

It needs a guid strong arm to beat it !

Over a low heat, melt the butter in a
large, heavy-bottomed saucepan. Add the
sugar and milk. Keep stirring until the
sugar has dissolved. Add the condensed
milk, turn the heat up a wee bitty and
bring to the boil awfy slowly. Turn
the heat down and let it simmer for 20
minutes. Test the mixture for hardness
after 18 minutes by dropping a wee drap
mixture from the spoon into a bowl of
cold water. If it turns into a soft ball
that you can pick up between your
fingers then it is time to remove the
mixture from the heat. Take off the heat
and Beat for 3 to 5 mins. Pour into a
baking tray and score into fingers.

DUnDEE
EDINBURGH ROCK

- 450 g/1 lb sugar
- 150 ml/¼ pint water
- ¼ tsp cream of tartar
- Food colouring
- Peppermint or lemon flavouring
- A little oil

Pour the sugar and water into a thick-bottomed saucepan and cook over a medium heat till the sugar has dissolved. Turn the heat up and, just before boiling point, add the cream of tartar. Boil the mixture until it reaches 'hard ball' consistency 120C/250F. Or, into a glass of cold water, drop a little of the mixture and when it forms a hard ball you will know that it has reached the correct temperature.

Divide the mixture into two — flavour and colour separately. Allow to cool slightly in oiled trays. Pull and fold the mixtures several times. Roll into a long log shape and cut into small lozenges. Leave to cool completely and store in an air-tight box.

Mushroom Ketchup

- 1.4 kg/3 ½ lbs mushrooms
- 50 g/2 oz salt
- A further 25g /1 oz salt per 150 ml/¼ pint of juice
- 5 cloves
- 7 g/ ¼ oz root ginger
- 7 g/ ¼ oz peppercorns
- Pinch of cayenne pepper

Break the mushrooms up into small pieces, place in a stoneware pan and sprinkle with salt. Let them stand for three days, frequently stirring and mashing them to cause the juice to flow. Strain and get all the juice possible from the mushrooms by adding pressure. To each quart of juice add 25 g/1 oz salt. Put the spices in a bag and boil with the mushrooms and juice for an hour, then strain. Bottle and cork.

Great for seasoning stocks and stews. Even use it like soy sauce.

Granpaw's Elderberry Wine

1.8 kg/4 lbs elderberries
3.7 litres/1 gallon water
1.8 kg/4 lbs sugar
50 g/1 oz fresh yeast
1 thick slice of toast
After ten days: 450 g/1 lb raisins

Remove the berries from the stalks (stripping with a fork might be easiest) and boil in the water for half an hour. Strain and cool the liquid in a brewing container. When the liquid is almost cold, add the sugar and mix thoroughly. Spread the fresh yeast on the slice of toast and drop this into the liquid. Cover the container loosely and leave it to stand for 10 days. After ten days, strain again and add 1 lb of raisins. Allow this to stand in your brewing container for six weeks. Strain again and decant into bottles — only once you are sure it has stopped fermenting — and cork.

Horace's Index

FOR THE PEOPLE

HUDSON'S SOAP

IN PACKETS EVERYWHERE

for washing up and cleaning down

why do

the nicest, tastiest meals, that have been a pleasure to cook, sometimes remain untasted by the clever housewife who prepared them? Very likely because she is already thinking, poor thing, of that stack of dirty plates and dishes that the feast will leave—of that eternal washing up that

women hate

so much that it even takes away the pleasure from their meals. If that is all that's on her mind she needn't worry. Just a shake of Hudson's Soap in the dishwater and her task is half done. Plates and dishes quickly become clear and shining, glasses sparkle, and hands don't get greasy. Hudson's is good for all household cleaning; but if you want to keep your appetite at dinner-time just remind yourself that there will be Hudson's to help you with the

washing up

R. S. HUDSON LIMITED, LIVERPOOL, WEST BROMWICH, AND LONDON

The Selkirk Grace

* * * * * * * * * *

Some hae meat and canna eat,

And some wad eat that want it;

But we hae meat, and we can eat,

Sae let the Lord be thankit.

* * * * * * * * * *

Miss TUX[FORD]

Lemon Essence			
Almond	do.		
Vanilla	do.	...	at 1/- "
Apple Green Colouring	...	at 6d.	"
Carmine	do.	...	at 6d. "
Yellow	do.	...	at 6d. "
Violet	do.	...	at 6d. "

Postage, 2d. extra.

All above prepared and recommended by the Authoress.

Useful and Inexpensive Utensils.

Cooling Tray for Cakes, Bread, etc. ... 1/- each
Postage 3d. extra

Straining Grid (for use in deep fat frying, or boiling fish and cauliflowers whole (see page 35) (Designed by myself) } 6" size 9d. each
Postage 2d. extra
8" size 1/3 each
Postage 3d. extra.

Whisk for beating Eggs, Cream, or Cake Mixture ... ... 6d. each
Postage, 1½d. extra

Finger Biscuit Cutter ... ... 4d. each
Per Post, 5½d.

Set of Icing Pump and Two Tubes ... 2/6
Per Post, 2/9

Palette Knives ... ... 2/- each
Per Post, 2/3

Méringue or Choux Pastry Tubes 7d. each
(Plain or Star Patterns) Per Post, 8d.

9in. Round Sandwich Cake Tins 1/3
(Loose Bottoms) Per Post, 1/7

6in. Square Slab Cake Tins... ... ... 1/-
(Loose Bottoms) Per Post, 1/4
(Recommended for Parkin, Genoa Cake, Raised Pie, etc.)

Imperial ½pt. (Gill) Aluminium Measure, 1/6 each
Per Post, 1/8

Address all communications :

Miss H. H. TUXFORD, M.C.A.,

"WESTWOOD," TATTERSHALL, LINCOLN.